[Type here]

ISBN-13:
978-1724295477

ISBN-10:
1724295470
Fifth Edition
Copyright © 2010, 2011, 2012, 2014, and 2018 Todd Kachinski

DRAG411's Ten Black Books

Book 1:	**DRAG411's "DRAG Bully, A Survivor's Guide"**
	Copyright © 2015 and 2018
Book 2:	**DRAG411's "Original DRAG Handbook"**
	Copyright © 2010, 2011, 2012, 2014, and 2018
Book 3:	**DRAG411's "Crown Me! Winning Pageants"**
	Copyright © 2013, 2014, and 2018
Book 4:	**DRAG411's "DRAG King Handbook"**
	Copyright © 2014 and 2018
Book 5:	**DRAG411's "DRAG Stories"**
	Copyright © 2011, 2014, and 2018
Book 6:	**DRAG411's "DRAG Mother, DRAG Father"**
	Copyright © 2012, 2014, and 2018
Book 7:	**DRAG411's "Spotlight Magazine"**
	Copyright © 2012 and 2018
Book 8:	**DRAG411's "DRAG Queen Guide"**
	Copyright © 2014 and 2018
Book 9:	Two Comedy Scripts:
	DRAG411's "Best Said Dead"
	Copyright © 2011, 2014, and 2018
	"Following Wynter"
	Copyright © 2012, 2014, and 2018
Book 10:	**DRAG411's "DRAG World"**
	Copyright © 2012 and 2018

From the best-selling author of "CommUnity of Transition,"
"Two Days Past Dead," The Novel and the sequel,
"Turn Around Bright Eyes, The DRAG Queen Killer,"
"Joey Brooks, The Show Must Go On,"
and "Waiting On God."

DRAG411's

The Official,
Original Handbook

5th Edition

I am not a fan of the term "drag" as applied across this entire art form, but until they find a single word "more accepting," I will have to use it. The drag community has helped me earn twenty LGBT world records. I created DRAG411 to document this form of entertainment. We are the world's largest organization for male, female, and androgynous impersonators with over 7,000 current or former impersonators in 32 countries.   The Infamous Todd Kachinski Kottmeier

(sic)

Latin adverb: thus"; in full: sic erat scriptum, thus was it written indicates DRAG411 transcribed the comments into this book exactly as found in the original source, complete with any erroneous or archaic spelling or other nonstandard presentation. We try to print the responses using the same words sent to us, ensuring the reader DRAG411 did not change the tone, reflection, or character of each response.

> **We print verbatim, without editing**
>
> **ver·ba·tim   vərˈbātəm/**
> **adverb: verbatim; adjective**
> **in exactly the same words as used originally.**

Go to our website at
Drag411.com
to locate any name listed
in any of the books
in our Ten Black Book series
and the details of each
book, entertainer,
and chapter.

Foreword

Steve and I did not charge anyone to be in this book. Our invitation was open and unconditional. To be on the contributing writers list, the person had to reply to only one of any of the 102 questions we slowly posted over four months in 2010 on the DRAG411 page on facebook.

Through the social network, we sent thousands of invitations across the country. Each invitation begged the recipient also to send out invitations to the performers they respected. Our hope was to reach everyone. It was the goal of this project to be all-inclusive. It was open for any male or female impersonator.

After we printed the handbook in 2011, we decided to donate 100% of the profits for five years to AIDS/Causes. We later designated many of the other DRAG411 books to the same cause for the first year.

Note: *Many of the readers of this book will read the words through jaded eyes. Many of readers take them personally. When you get to the sections of the book you totally disagree, remember that the information arrives from hundreds of thousands of words shared by other performers.*

If you get to the Anger section of the book and you do not see any correlation of reality compared to the words we typed, consider yourself lucky. Consider your life fortunate to have lived in this environment without sharing pain, anger, hatred, jealousy, and sarcasm. For those words, we only wrote to those making a difference in improving the respect of this craft.

Some of you will disagree with our viewpoints.

Front Cover
Above Title

First Row
1 Mis Sadistic
2 Amy DeMilo
3 Beverly LaSalle
4 Dmentia Divinyl
5 Mr Kenneth Blake
6 Kitty D'Meaner
7 Kiki LaFlare Santangilo
8 Ineeda Twat

Second Row
1 Dee Gregory
2 Lady Tajma Hall (RIP)
3 Maxine Padlock
4 Glitz Glam
5 Patricia Grand
6 Tatum Michelle
7 Felicia Fox
8 Coco Labelle

Third Row
1 TotiYanah Diamond
2 Tiffani Middlesexx
3 Jade Daniels
4 Miss Gigi
5 Teri Courtney (RIP)
6 Ima Twat
7 Trixie LaRue
8 Jade Jolie

Front Cover
Below Title

Fourth Row
1 Alexis De La Mar
2 Patricia Mason
3 Cathy Craig

[Type here]

4 Rhyana Vorhman Vorhman
5 Conundrum
6 Melody Mayheim
7 Madisyn de la Mer
8 Naomi Wynters

Fifth Row
1 PurrZsa Kyttyn
2 LeeAnna Love
3 Adora
4 Pussy LeHoot
5 Esme Russell
6 Joey Brooks
7 Coco Montrese
8 Alexis Mateo

Sixth Row
1 Pandora DeStrange
2 Kori Stevens
3 Champagne T Bordeaux
4 Nicole Paige Brooks
5 Jade Sotomayor
6 Anastasia Fallon
7 Blair Michaels
8 Miss Conception

Back Cover First Row
1 RuPaul
2 Jaeda Fuentes
3 Misty Eyez
4 Afeelya Bunz
5 Alisa Summers
6 Allure
7 Amanda Bone
8 Amanda Love

Second Row
1 Barbra Seville
2 Ana Rexia
3 Ashleigh Cooley

4 Babette Schwartz
5 Bailey St. James
6 Barbra Herr
7 Brianna Lee
8 Brittany Moore

Third Row
1 Cartier Paris
2 CoCo St. James
3 Daphne Ferraro
4 Deva DaVyne
5 Diedra Windsor Walker
6 Eunyce Raye
7 Ginger Minj
8 Horchata

Fourth Row
1 Jade Shanell
2 Jenna Chambers Tisdale
3 Jessica Jade
4 Jocelyn Summers
5 Kamden Wells
6 Katrina Starr
7 Krystal Leight
8 Lacey Lynn Taylors

Fifth Row
1 Lady Clover Honey
2 LaKeisha Pryce
3 Leigh Shannon
4 Lisa Carr
5 Lola Honey
6 Gilda Golden
7 Melissa Morgan
8 Monique Michaels

Sixth Row
1 Mystique Summers
2 Nairobi V. D'Viante
3 Nova Starr

4 Ororo
5 Patrice Knight
6 Polly Funk Chanel
7 Rickie Lee
8 Shae Shae LaReese

Seventh Row
1 Shugah Caine
2 Stephanie Stuart
3 Stormy Vain
4 Makayla Rose Devine
5 Venus D Lite
6 Wendy G. Kennedy
7 BukkakeBlaque London St. James
Dedication

**Contributing Impersonator adding their
Wisdom in this Handbook include…**

D -Dedications
P -Photographer

Ada Buffet
Adora (D) Friends and Family
Adrian Leigh
Afeelya Bunz Alisa Summers (D) Florida Entertainment Group, Toby Brees
(P) Kristofer Reynolds Alba Summers
Alanna Divine
Alexis De La Mer (D) Ariel Sin Claire
Alexis Mateo (D) Luz and Iris
Alex Serpa
Allure
Amanda Bone (D) Karen & Desiree
Amanda Love (D) Summer Clearence & Natalie Small
Amy DeMilo (D) Anne Lee & Marty Curtin (P) Visual FX Studios
Anastaia Fallon (D) My Parents and Sister (P) Christina J. Bourque
Astasnaia Rexia (D) Andrea Morgan & Cathy Kelly
Angel gLamar
Angela Dodd
Anita Cox
April Fresh
Ashleigh Cooley

Aurora Sexton
Babette Schwartz
Bailey St. James
Barbra Herr
Barbra Seville
Beverly LaSalle (D) Mis Sadistic & Dana Douglas
BJ Stephens
Blair Michaels (D) Brad Michaels & Kerri Lake
Brandon M. Caten
Brianna Lee
Brittany Moore
Brookyln Bisette
Bukkake Blaque London St. James (D) Nove Kane & Blowme Bubbles
Cartier Paris (D) Lisha Paris & Envy Van Michaels
Cathy Craig (D) Ted Larson & Tiny Tina
Champagne T. Bordeaux (D) Paulette Christian & Keith Bolster (P) Visual FX
StudiosCherry Darling
Christina Paris
CoCo LaBelle
CoCo Montrese
CoCo St. James
Conundrum (D) My Fans & Supporters
Crystal Belle (D) Studio 13 Family and the Belles
Daniel Murphy
Danika Fierce
Daphne Ferraro
Dasha Nicole
Dee Gregory (D) Mr. Rickie Lee & Ana Cristy Garcia
Deva DaVyne
Diamond Dunhill
Diedra Windsor Walker (D) Stephanie Richards and my Arkansas Sisters
Dmentia Divinyl/Eva LaDeva (D) Harris Glen Milstead & Vincent J.
Wiercinski
Echo Dazz
Esme Russell (D) Renee Rodriguez from Renee's & Tiffany Middlesexxx (P)
Visual FX Studios
Estelle Rivers
Eunyce Raye (D) Jewel Soles (P) Charles Snavely
Felica Fox (D) Chelsea Night Club & My Family
Felina Cashmere
Geraldine Queen Cabaret
Ginger Minj (D) Mother & Husband
Glitz Glam (D) To my sister Tressa Love and Daisy Deadpetals

Gilda Golden (D) Kim Ross & Roxanne Russell
Horchata
Ima Twat (D) Ineeda Twat & Bette Davis
Ineeda Twat (D) Ima Twat and Miss Holly Girl
Jade Daniels (D) Nicole Paige Brooks & Doug Baker
Jade Jolie (D)
Jade Shanell (D) Shawna Roze & My Parents
Jade Sotomayo (D) My DRAG Mother & Noemi Pena (P) Norman Dillon
Jaeda Fuentes (D) Kori Stevens & S'Myra Sky-Banks
Jami Micheals
Jay Santana
Jeffrey Powell
Jenna Chambers Tisdale (D) Sydney & Camero
Jessica Jade
Jocelyn Summers
Jodie Holliday
Joey Brooks (D) Friends and Family (P) Loc Robertson
Joshua Myers
J.P. Patrick
Juwanna Jackson
Kamden Wells
Katrina Starr (D) Jason and Paris
Kenny Braverman
Khrystal Leight
Kier Sarkesian
Kiki LaFlare Santangilo
Kitty D'Meaner (D) Theresa A Quigley & Vivian Lynn D'Maples
Kori Stevens (D) Friends and Fans
Krystal Amore Adonis
Lacey Lynn Taylors (D) Vivianne Lee Taylors and Zachary T
Lady Clover Honey (D) Lovari
Lady Sabrina
Lady TaJma Hall
Lakeisha Pryce (D) Suzanne Sugarbaby and Sasha Stephens
LeeAnna Love (D) Mother Joanna Haslam & Miss Dee Dee Monroe
Leigh Shannon
Lisa Carr
Lola Honey (D) My Mother Keshia & Abel
Madisyn De La Mer (D) To my DRAG family & my birth mother Nikki
Makayla Rose Devine (D) Cece Absolutely Divine
Maxine Padlock (Maxi Pad) (D) Jane Parrella
Melissa Morgan
Melody Mayheim

Michael Wilson
Mike Astermon-Glidden
Mis Sadistic (D) Shirleena and JoJo
Miss Conception
Miss Gigi (D) Nina Bunting and My fans
Mr. Kenneth Blake (D) The Writers and Contributors of this book
Misty Eyez
Monique Michaels (D) My mother and Jason
Myah Monroe
Mystique Summers
Nairobi V. D'Viante
Naomi D-Lish
Naomi Wynters (D) Justin Daniel Duncan & Dion Trala
Nicole Paige Brooks
Nikki Dynamite
Nova Starr
Ororo
Patrica Grand (D)
Patricia Knight (D) Kim Ross & Crystlas
Patrica Mason (D) Eryka Knowles & Christina Mason
Pandora DeStrange
Penelope Reigns (D) My late Mother & ChiChi Lalique
Polly FunkChanel (D) Burlesque & Cabaret Social Club & April Showers (P)
Rick Taylor
Phiore Star Liemont
Purrzsa Kyttyn (D) Rodney Gibson & LaLa
Pussy LeHoot
Raquel Payne
Rhyana Vorhman Vorhman (D) Dusti Howe & Alicia Markstone
Rickie Lee (D) Edward Kramer & Alfred Fullard
Rusti Fawcett
Scarlett Fever
Selina Kyle
Shae Shae LaReese
Shealita Babay
Shugah Caine
Stephanie Roberts
Stephanie Stuart
Stormy Vain (D) Stevie Starfyre & Nancy
Summer Breeze
Sybil Storm
Tabatha Lovall
Tatum Michelle (D) Scott Pierce & Matt Scandin

Teri Courtney (D) Kim y Rosario & Lady Catira Reyes
Tiffani Middlesexx (D) Darcel Stevens & Rosey Mayes
Timm McBride
Toni Davyne
TotiYanah Diamond
Trixie LaRue (D) My Biscuit Sisters
Trixie Pleasures (D) Aneal Pleasures and Leslie Scott
Vegas Platinum
Venus D Lite (D) Gay Youth
Vivika D'Angelo (D) Angie & Mama Cook
Wendel Duppert
Wendy G. Kennedy

Name the performers without checking on
DRAG411.com

Chapters

Bonus Chapter:
Why Me, Harvey Milk?

"You cannot expect society to treat you with dignity as long as you allow other performers to disrespect each other."

The Infamous Todd Kachinski Kottmeier

"If you don't love yourself, how in the hell you gonna love somebody else?"

RuPaul

❋ ❋ ❋

Chapter One

Relationships

Makeup has a distinct smell recognized by a man raised around many sisters or perhaps a sloppy mother. For a gay man, the smell of makeup is often like the telltale signs of a kitty litter box, of a cat owner trying to hide their feline child. This chapter has nothing to do with female impersonators. It is a tribute to the secret army of benefactors that complement performers spiritually, emotionally and often without reserve.

Creating this chapter taught me more about myself than any chapter in this book. Don't get me wrong, I am not a female impersonator. The thought of it not only scares me. "Me in a dress" would terrify my neighborhood.

Do not get me wrong, I am not one of the men that have a female impersonator on his resume of relationships (1). Not because I did not want them, but most likely most of them were smart enough to not want me. Researching this chapter consolidated many of the stereotypes I had set in my brain from a long history of working with and employing these performers.

In this chapter, it is not the strengthening of the stereotypes that I wish to explore with much detail. I want to spend time discussing the revelations of what makes their relationships with men far beyond expected conforms of my stereotypes and of my preset rationalization of their relationships.

(1). Updated: Dated Angel gLamar in 2012 for a year. We both barely survived.

Now back to writing this book. Dating someone that performs as a female impersonator takes a special man. He has to be mentally alert to handle situations where many people would fail. He has to be able to explore life through his boyfriend's eyes, without reservation and judgment. He has to be willing to spare closet space, room around the sink, with his best pay off at the end of the night... is seeing the light in his boyfriend's eyes reflecting the happiness he shares in that relationship. I lived in a home with more sisters than any man should ever have to tolerate, run by a matriarchal grandmother that created my mother, that ran our home. The smell of estrogen in the air would choke you as the smell of a cadre of females past puberty shared the same menstrual cycle. The side benefit of becoming a gay man was the knowledge I would no longer have to tolerate a cluttered sink of blow dryers, curling irons, hair spray cans, and random bottles of makeup scattered across the bathroom with jubilee.

The exciting part of becoming a gay man was no longer having to tolerate drying pantyhose dangling down from the shower, having to watch my sisters practice dance routines, and listening to the same damned songs over and over again. As a gay man, I fit the stereotype of thinking, "I would never date a female impersonator. If I wanted to date a girl, I would have remained straight."

There are two types of people, I thought, that date female impersonators. The straight man that believes that dating a female impersonator justifies him still being straight. The other is a mild, meek, and submissive gay man tagging behind the performer, carrying seven cases of changing clothes and makeup.

This is the average stereotype of the average gay man, but this is a book about exploring averages. The word average, by its true nature, determines that 99 % of the people do not agree with the conclusion. The math on that determines that 50% of each response is either for or against the conclusion, henceforth the word average.

When I was younger, thinking I was a straight man, hanging out with friends in cleverly titled gay bars like Old Plantation, Rene's, El Goya, and The Carousel I found myself fascinated by the groupies hanging around Kim Ross, Tiffani Middlesexx, Joey Brooks, and Gilda Golden. I am confident my stereotype developed during those informative years.

A male perspective forces us to believe someone surrounded by enthusiastic adoration cannot help themselves but to be sexually tempted. We watch growing up, a legion of movie stars along with rock and roll performers destroy their relationships and marriages, in search of sexual gratification of someone tossing themselves at their feet.

It would not be a far reach to believe my mind assumes this behavior repeats in the gay culture. It would not be a far reach in my mind to believe many of the people in the throng of admirers 'were guys getting sexual gratification from bedding cross-dressers and transsexuals.'

During that period of my life, the group of female impersonators around me encompassed performers that were boys off stage, some were prostitutes, and a few actually returned the adoration of the straight man with their own fetish of being excited by landing a man that claimed he was straight.

The second groups of DRAG boyfriends were these meek and mild mannered men scurrying through the bar behind the performers. Maybe part of my stereotype had to do with my own over the top, Infamous Todd persona. I knew that no self-respecting performer would want to date a person like me, just the thought of us rolling through the grass chasing a misplaced microphone seemed silly for both parties.

In reading the 199,021 words archived by facebook for this project, I discovered that 38.88% of the performers declared that their significant others did not realize they performed as a female when they first met.

Another Comedy Play By Best Selling Writer
Todd Kachinski~Kottmeier with Steve Hammond

PurrZsa Kyttyn, *"When I first met my boyfriend, we were both dressed as boys. I told him that I did DRAG, and he was like 'okay'. After the show, he was more like, 'what the f*ck'. He asked me what I was doing, and I told him I did not know. His response, "I can tell."*

Jocelyn Summers, *"Unfortunately, my last three husbands had known of Jocelyn first. I believe that hurt the relationship because Jocelyn is not me, but a persona that I created for the show. I was Jason, a complex person."*

Selina Kyle, *"Actually I met him while I was in DRAG, then he met me that Saturday out of face and he had no idea that we had met days earlier."*

The average long-term gay relationship is only sixteen months(1) long. I found this figure quite alarming, until I realized that determining this factor required the input of relationships that barely made it through the year. Television social norms, teaching us gay men are unable to function in relationships. The purpose of this book has nothing to do with the equality of gay marriage, but the quality of relationships formed with a female impersonator.

It is only fair to note for the purpose of this book, that the version of female impersonator I am addressing has little to do with transgender or transsexual alliance, but performers dressing as a female to entertain. The number that floored me out of the 21,018 comments posted had to do with one subject.

Relationships:
How long have you been in your current relationship?

Looking past the blow dryer on the sink, the makeup scattered through the cupboards, these relationships flourish past adversity, complications, and the stigma of social norms. The two-year countdown to breakup that plagues the average gay man falls to the side as the performers flood the questionnaire heralding their eleven-year average.

Babette Schwartz, *"We have been together for twenty-four years. He is my biggest athletic supporter."*

BJ Stephens, *"I am truly blessed to be with my husband twenty-three years. He supports me, helps me with my performances, is my best sounding board, and has an objective viewpoint. Can you tell I love him?"*

Amy DeMilo, *"I have been in 3 relationships, now single and loving it."* [Note: Many of these performers are now in current relationships again.]

(1). Long-term relationship averages were based on math of couples together twelve months or longer.

Pandora DeStrange, *"My last two relationships lasted eight years, but I am close to both of them. They are my FAMILY! If someone knows all your dirt you should keep them close in case you have to choke the f*ck out of them."*

Wendy G. Kennedy, *"I am married to a beautiful loving and caring woman. Her name is Arden. She's my biggest supporter and number one fan. We've been married since 2003 and we love each other very much."*

Rusti Fawsett, *"He is the Ying to my Yang; twenty years."*

Summer Breeze, *"I have been with the same wonderful man for twenty-nine years. He does all the cooking; the only thing I know how to make is reservations."*

The amazing part of collecting information for this chapter is 7.27% of the performers were able to hide the fact they were performing as women on stage to the person they were dating during the relationship. Equally surprising, 7.18% of the participants noted their relationships stopped after their partner started performing too.

The thousands of responses stated, performing added complications to the relationship, but "made the relationship stronger."

The complexities of entering the relationship did not reflect in the statistics of "single vs. in a relationship" compared to the average gay man. Of those polled, 47.63% said they were currently in a relationship; a higher success rate than the 46% of gay men not involved with a performer.

A person dating a female impersonator is required to take a more active role in the career of the person they are dating. It is hard to avoid the commitment it takes dating someone practicing routines at home, cannot drive down the road without lip synching the words to a song, constantly parades outfits back and forth throughout the day, spends endless hours on the telephone arranging performances, and finally goes to bed smelling of grease paint.

No matter what profession a person selects for their life, a waiter, a teacher, a hair stylist, or even the president of a bank, would they ever contemplate asking their partner to be completely involved in their career?

A female impersonator has to ask their partner to reach far beyond their wallet, past mental limitations of stereotypes created over years of social reform, and to give them unconditional support.

Only 32% of straight households contain a partner not supporting their spouse's job. In the GLBTQ community, 42% of the relationships do not support the activities of their partner. It is incredible to learn 93.87% of the partners in a performer's relationship offer them positive support.

Being supportive mentally, financially and spiritually does not obligate the performer's spouse to be a meek and mild person toting the wheeled Samsonite. Each person defines their relationship with their partner differently, yet a surprising 73.46% stated their partner assisted during actual performances.

Monique Michaels, *"My partner helps me when he is needed. I don't ever have to ask, he's just there."*

Ada Buffet, *"My partner packs my bag, does set-up then break down, operates my makeup station, creates music CD's, whatever I need. He just does it without asking. He knows what I need and when I need it."*

Patricia Mason, *"He was backstage during my first pageant. He reluctantly came back to assist me getting into a gown. He looked around and saw naked performers who had work done and was quite mortified. He doesn't come backstage any more, but is still my #1 fan in the audience."*

Name the performers without checking on DRAG411.com

"I believe no subculture of mankind represents the goodness in charity more than DRAG impersonators. As a group, they have cultivated a long history of fighting for what is right by financially empowering every cause without condition."

The Infamous Todd Kachinski Kottmeier

❆❆❆

Chapter Two

Charity

The chapter on charity represents four percent of this entire book, but it is just as important as saying my heart only represents four percent of my body.

It was not the spirit of the performers attracting me to this project. It was not their talent, their conversations, or even their humor. To a person like me, I could purchase all of this from them with a dampened wet dollar at the local bar. To think of a female impersonator as a performer, of a 3-minute act they lip synch on stage, not only cheapens that person, but also makes the patron illiterate to his own history.

In accumulating the notes to write this book, no section brought tears to my eyes more than my ignorance to their charity. My resource material for this book totaled over sixteen thousand pages. Of those sixteen thousand pages, I compiled and assimilated 102 surveys on GLBTQ (gay, lesbian, bi, transgender, and/ or questioning) history, only one word remained on the top of all the lists.

Stonewall

At 1:20 am, Saturday, June 29, 1969, in a small bar in Greenwich Village the face of the gay movement began. It's unfair to call Stonewall Inn a bar, as most people are totally unaware that the business did not have a license to serve alcohol. I do not plan to spend the next twenty pages re-examining Stonewall, for there are far better books dedicated to this subject.

Flash forward

Several years ago, Tampa, Florida was having one of its last indoor gay pride events. I sat near the Convention Center, which the organizers set up for after-parade-activities, watching the parade as it concluded downtown. Around me were about thirty conservative gay men, for whatever definition it may carry. One by one, I listened as fellow gay revelers complained of the local television network focusing attention on the female impersonators filtered throughout the event.

"Why must they show the most bizarre people as a representation of *the gays*?"

I repeatedly heard this whispered across the sidewalks of Hillsborough County. For a moment, I felt the spirit of what it must have been like in the spring of 1969, hiding in a seedy room drinking water from glasses barely washed in two bus tubs sitting behind the bar top at Stonewall Inn.

I thought about what it must have been like, to be "like these guys around me" hiding in Stonewall as the police poured through the front door. I know where these men would have been. They would have been running out the back door, scattering down the streets; they would have been trying to blend back into their neighborhood.

I know this to be true, because I was the President of the Young Republican's Club in college, and I thought everything has its place in time. Seldom do things change by being apathetic to the conditions around you.

On this July summer evening in 1969, there were people far stronger in character then me. I was lucky on this still quiet night knowing there were people far smarter than me, and unlike the guys standing at the parade route in Tampa, I realized people like me and people like us, owe our rights to be standing on visibly on sidewalks to female impersonators.

There are only two things that scare me in life, a pissed off dog and a pissed off DRAG queen. I cannot picture the expression on the New York Police Department's face as throngs of angry men in dresses tore the city apart.

So there I sat, inside my room, looking at 102 survey questions defining the DRAG community and its representation to "the gays." I realized the name Stonewall owed its very existence in time to the people with whom I share this book.

Not every female impersonator is "pretty", but before my statement offends a person, they should remember, not every person is pretty. It is not a wild assumption to believe some of the entertainers are not purposely reaching to be pretty. Prettiness is not the primary goal, as a performer's primary goal and obligation is to entertain. It is why we call them entertainers and not models. Once they work out the details of performing, than they can negotiate prettiness.

Not every person who puts on a dress has the ability to stand on the stage to pull off a routine worthy of an invite back to a venue. It takes much more than blush, eyeliner and a good wig to entertain a crowd. It is the spirit and dedication of any entertainer to win the crowd's attention.

Stonewall is the first national event hosted by this generosity, by a group of pissed-off DRAG queens. It could be argued Stonewall was their first non-charitable event for gay equality.

Every thirty-seven hours another gay publication hits the street in the United States. A common thread, far past the advertising to consume alcohol in each of these periodicals, is charity still rules the GLBTQ community Few straight publications dispensed by thousands of publishers throughout the United States offer more space dedicated to helping others less fortunate.

Breast Cancer, Homelessness, Teen Runaways, Suicides, Drug Intervention, HIV Awareness, and a host of other charities fight for the reader's attention. Each advertisement is done by a slick graphic artist, typesetters, and marketing departments. Periodicals have page after page of venues and businesses hosting events. The common thread through the pages falls upon the DRAG community.

In 2009,
For every $10.00 earned in venues for
GLBTQ causes, $8.82 came through the assistance
Of male and female impersonators.

Stop for a moment and let the impact of this huge figure sink in before you read another word in this book.

The number is defined by unconditional support by thousands of performers spending **744,368 hours working for free** to catch your attention. They spend their gas and evenings, with no financial reimbursement, to volunteer their time, to do the right thing, for the right reasons.

From Phoenix to Seattle, to Albany to Key West, is a legion of people fighting for our causes, earning almost one hundred thirty two million dollars, often one dollar at a time.

Jessica Jade, *"I've probably done twenty non-profit fundraiser shows this year and have another tonight. My persona started as something for charity and will always be that."*

Jade Shanell, *"I don't know. I never really kept count because I love doing charity shows. Anything for a good cause. I will be there with heels on."*

Rhyana Vorhman, *"I do dozens of shows for charity. I feel better than when I do a paid performance."*

Nikki Dynamite, *"I do everything I'm invited to. It's a great experience and it helps the community."*

Cherry Darling, *"Quite a few. Not only does this allow you to showcase your talents in areas you have not performed in yet, but also gives a sense of pride that you are contributing to a good cause. Oh my God! I am such a saint! Saint Cherry of the Maybelline order."*

Mr. Kenneth Blake, *"With my current show schedule it can be difficult these days, but I try and do as many as I can. Around ten. Not as many as I have in the past, sadly."*

Rusti Fawcett, *"I do one a month, and more when asked."*

Eunyce Raye, *"At least twelve. I am one of several performers who participate in DRAG bingo once a month to raise money for AIDS."*

LaKeisha Pryce, *"I do the majority of my shows a year for non-profits because I have lost loved ones. I am big on making a difference in someone's life for the better."*

Anastasia Rexia, *"As many as I can. Like my mother always told me 'It's nice to be important, but it's more important to be nice.' Giving back is one of the nicest things I can think of."*

Afeelya Bunz, *"Eighty-five percent of my performances are fundraisers for non-profits."*

Monique Michaels, *"When I started, I did over 100 in my first year. But, now, with work and show demands, not nearly as many. I try to make sure I contribute at least six to ten per year or more if time allows. I think it's an amazing thing to give back and use your voice and talent to do so."*

Kitty D'Meanor, *"This being my first year as a female impersonator, I have done several non-profit events. I've taken part in probably eight or ten. I enjoy doing things for a cause. It gives me an even larger sense of pride in what I do."*

"Those living a life without charity,
Live a life of greed."
The Infamous Todd Kachinski Kottmeier

Fun Facts

Note: 91% replied the same five movies!

Top Five
DRAG Movies

Too Wong Foo (43%)

Pricilla, Queen Of The Desert (13%)

<tied> Bird Cage and Torch Song Trilogy (11%)

Wigstock (4%)

<tied> Sordid Lives and Connie & Carla (4%)

Leaving 9% for everyone else...

Name the performers without checking on DRAG411.com

Hint: (Second Photo) She bought the very first The Original, Official DRAG Handbook

"I've dedicated my career to fighting the mundane. My hope is that my career will be a shining example to children everywhere that life is more meaningful when you are not afraid to see all colors of the rainbow."

RuPaul

❀ ❀ ❀

Chapter Three

Mother's Pretty Dress

G.I. Joe, a big bright yellow Tonka dump truck filled with sand sitting in the driveway, sixteen flattened matchbox cars mutilated by a passing train, a small black bag containing 42 marbles, 3 boulders and one steely.

The definition of a small boy is often the character our society places on how we represent adolescence. Growing up, few Americans are preview to Beaver Cleaver picking up his mother's pretty Sunday dress and placing it over his head to dance in front of a mirror. The stories straight and gay men both share, of trying a dress on for the first time, far exceeds Halloween enlightenment.

Deva DaVyne, *"The first time I dressed up was back in Middle School. I was home alone and went into my mother's closet and decided to play dress up. I remember my Mom walking in on me in her clothes and high heels and all she told me was that if I scuffed her floor, she would scuff my butt."*

Alisa Summers, *"It was never a dress. I was all about shoes. Whether it was my mother's or my grandmothers', I was all about some heels. There are pictures of me as a child, probably around four years old, in heels and hats. I'm sure if you ask my mother, she'd be happy to share them."*

Babette Schwartz, *"I was four years old. There is a picture of me wearing a half slip and pearls while twirling around the front yard."*

Felina Cashmere; Lady Tajma Hall; Vivika D'Angelo, *"My mother used to dress me as a girl."*

Alanna Divine, *"Fifteen years old. I had watched a Mae West movie and thought 'damn, this bitch is getting all the attention.' I went and found my mother's evening gown and put it on with her heels...ugh! The definition of the word 'hot mess'."*

Kiki LaFlare Santangilo, *"Sophomore year of college. I started watching RuPaul's DRAG Race on LOGO and thought 'Hey, I love makeup, I love performing...I think I can do that!' I put on a dress, did my makeup, put on a wig, slipped on some heels, and never looked back."*

I tried very hard to eliminate most of the comments on the survey using the word Halloween; because I believe, even my grandfather may have put on a wig to pretend to be a silly little girl. There is a big difference between being a boy, on a lark, placing a dress over his head for a moment, compared to the little boy placing a dress over his head and freaks out because he doesn't know the right shoes to go with his ensemble. The second boy is more concerned about the accessories for the outfit he now has placed over his head. The participants of this survey strongly fall into the latter group, which motivated me to ask them what brought that excitement to a continued pace.

Ada Buffet, *"It all started as a way to get into the bars. At that time DRAGs were not usually carded on entry. I did it to gain entry as a 'walk-around' queen, then eventually when I was old enough, I started entering competitions."*

Misty Eyez, *"From nine to twelve years old, but then got really Christian and didn't do it again until after my senior year of college, and that was when I knew I had to be a queen."*

Champagne T. Bordeaux, *"I can't say I ever liked it. I just needed the outside world to relate to me the way I could understand. That was at age 7. The DRAG of it all became enjoyable around the age of twenty when I won my first big competition."*

Mis Sadistic, *"Fifteen years old at the Ice Palace on Fire Island. I saw Connie Francis coming across the deck. I was mesmerized by this man who looked just like her. I stayed for the DRAG show. I was so busy talking to the show girls that I missed the last ferry home. This was a defining moment in my life. It was then that I knew I wanted to be a DRAG queen."*

Jami Michaels, *"At nineteen years old, a little late by most standards, but my now ex-boyfriend hung with female impersonators. He assumed that he* *could do makeup by association...not true. I looked a mess, but you couldn't tell me any different at the time."*

Geraldine Queen Cabaret, *"At twenty-four years old I decided to follow my heart. I told my sister that I wasn't just a gay guy, it was deeper than that. I asked her to help me by encouraging me to not repress myself anymore."*

Joey Brooks, *"I won a talent show at El Goya in Tampa, Florida. I loved the attention I was able to command from the audience."*

Patricia Knight, *"Age nineteen; I was in the Army in Germany. Some friends dared me to wear this hideous wig. I put it on and they said I looked like Tina Turner without makeup. At that point I decided I wanted to be a DRAG queen."*

Ineeda Twat, *"Sister Ima started earlier than sister Ineeda. Sister Ineeda was in her late twenty's when she first put on the makeup and dress for a talent contest at Rocky's Pub in Clearwater, Florida. From that moment on, I loved the attention.*

In the imagination of our youth, we live in a magical world. Left alone we can be Peter Pan, in a pool we can become Aqua Man. Lost in the woods as a child, we have the opportunity to be Robinson Crusoe. It has few limitations and confines.

Unfortunately, the world we live in our minds very rarely relates to reality. We grow up to discover few of us will actually walk on the moon, ride on the back of a fire truck, or be a cowboy chasing down a wild Indian. The best games we play as children are the games we play alone, until one day someone enters our imaginary world.

Naomi Wynters, *"The first time someone saw me as a girl, I was 19 years old. Some of my DRAG queen friends were sitting around trying to get me into DRAG. I wasn't feeling it. Finally, they talked me into it."*

Maxine Padlock, *"I was originally Cher Candy. One day I dressed up all out fishy to go to my mother's house. I knocked and started walking in past her. She was like 'Can I help you?' I said, 'Ma?' and she was like OMG! She actually thought I was one of her boyfriend's hoochie mama's. That was a good one. And, she wanted to wear my hair..."*

Conundrum, *"First off, anytime a boy/man dresses as a girl/woman, it always directs a lot of attention towards that person. Unfortunately, I don't remember when or who saw me the first time, but I do remember trying on* *makeup one day. Someone rang my doorbell, so I tried to wash it off so fast and answer the door that I didn't completely remove the makeup. I remember the question 'are you wearing makeup?' Needless to say, I was a little embarrassed that I was caught."*

Name the performers without checking on DRAG411.com

Venus D Lite, *"I was eighteen and the first person to see me was my boyfriend. He looked at me and said 'Oh hell No!'"*

Jade Jolie, *"My first roommate heard me clucking in my shoes on the tile. Luckily they were completely supportive and even pushed me to continue further."*

Lacey Lynn Taylors, *"The first time anyone saw me dressed in DRAG was at the Beaux Arts Ball in Lexington, Kentucky. I was twenty years old and I looked a mess as far as DRAG goes, but I didn't know that then. My friends didn't recognize me and I had all the straight guys fooled."*

Pussy LeHoot, *"As a pre-teen, I was always mistaken for a girl. It was 1972. I had typical long boy hair bleached from the summer sun. I was thin and was tan and I looked like a girl. I rode my bike up to the corner store one night and this twenty-four year old guy started talking to me. He thought I* *was a girl. We ended up pulling around the corner in his truck and I masturbated him. I didn't even know what I was doing really, he showed me what to do, and when he "came" I didn't know what it was. He said, 'that's what makes babies.' He kissed me and asked me to meet him the next night, and I did. He never touched me. I sometimes wonder if he knew I was a boy. Who cares? I was hooked!"*

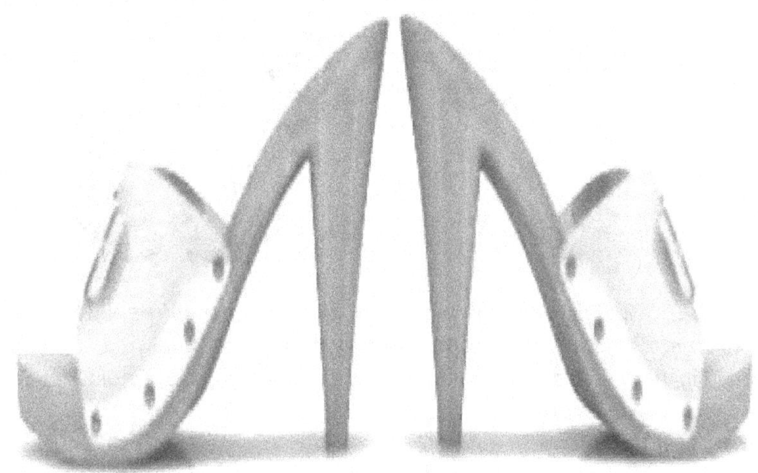

At thirteen, a young Jewish boy goes into the woods to earn his Bar Mitzvah to come back a man. In this book, I believe, the distinction for a female impersonator should be when he has the courage to walk into a retail shop to purchase his first article of female clothing.

Horchata, *"I was eighteen years old the first time I purposely purchased girls attire. I purchased pantyhose and was scared as hell. It took me an hour to go to check out."*

Amanda Bone, *"Eighteen. My Mom and I went to buy two wigs. We asked the lady if she had anything that would make me look less like a football player."*

Ororo Summers, *"By myself when I was twenty. I was so scared I didn't want to take anyone with me, and I didn't know my sizes. I didn't want people to think I was weird, so I didn't want to use the dressing rooms to see if they fit. I was a mess. I remember making up a story to an Associate, who was a hot guy, that I was trying to buy clothes for my "twin" sister and we were just about the same sizes."*

Jaeda Fuentes, *"I first did it when I was eighteen. It wasn't really that big of a deal to me. My best friend and I went and did it together and had a lot of fun doing it too. We got some cute outfits, and all the employees loved seeing us try things on."*

Glitz Glam, *"Twenty-one years old, it all happened fast. I went shopping at the Swap Shop in Ft. Lauderdale, Florida. The Indian guy who ran the place wouldn't let me try anything on."*

Lee Anna Love, *"Twenty-one. I went to the local mall during day time hours. The girls in the shop loved it so much that they were handing clothes over the dressing room door for me to try on and model for them. Mind you, I was dressed as a boy when I went in."*

Each week the television screen danced with Carrie Bradshaw on Sex and the City as she twirled around her living room in pure delight over some fashion find she discovered on her walk back from work. I asked the performers if they found wearing women's clothing as, "exciting."

Alexis Mateo, *"The chance to be someone else excited me. I love to impersonate women in the music industry."*

Diedra Windsor Walker, *"Oh I loved furs and I loved the jewels and I loved being glamorous. I wanted, and still love, the 1940's and 1950's style. It's so glamorous and just fabulous. I love the hair styles...the Victory Buns.*

Jocelyn Summers, *"Nothing, it is tight and binding and uncomfortable, especially the shoes."*

Jade Shanell, *"Being in DRAG is just fun. You get to bring a character to life and get people around you to have fun too. But, I do admit, I am a shoe whore, the higher the better. If they make it, I can walk in it."*

Kori Stevens, *"There isn't anything exciting about wearing women's clothing. The exciting thing is being able to entertain audiences. It's uncomfortable."*

Alisa Summers, *"I really enjoy the shopping aspect of it. I am definitely addicted to spending money. Then, taking the things you bought and piecing them together to create a final look is the best."*

Name the performers without checking on
DRAG411.com

Most straight men believe female impersonators are men living their lives wearing dresses. The average female impersonator dressing up in public will not buy this book. Though many DRAG performers are transgender, never should a person assume transgender people are DRAG queen. One is far from the other, and often compared with hateful content. The average female impersonator inside this book is a performer. The purpose of them placing on a dress, as proved by the 62.5% respondents stating, "They only wear a dress on stage" to perform.

Arguably, the other 37.5% could possibly be cross-dressers, but not the purpose of this book on entertainers. Transgender books, as my compilation resource guide, "CommUnity in Transition," is more adapted for better understanding.

Diamond Dunhill, *"I'm a boy in the day, girl at night. No additions, no subtractions, and I have stood by that since day one, September 19, 1999."*

Kiki LaFlare Santangilo, *"I dress in DRAG only when I'm*
performing. When my song is over, I'm backstage and I leave the club as a man. DRAG is for entertainment purposes only for me. I've had several men ask if I would dress as a woman all the time so we could date, but I turned them down. I'm not into that."

Patricia Mason, *"I have absolutely no desire to be a woman. I enjoy being masculine and being a man. I do enjoy putting on a show, creating a character and bringing that person to life. Being a female illusionist takes me from one extreme to the other."*

Toni DaVyne, *"I go out a lot in DRAG to promote myself and network and bring in new people to the clubs. I only shop for DRAG IN DRAG, because I feel like that is the only way you'll know for sure if it'll fit right and look good and with the look you're going for."*

Esme Russell, *"I have lived as a female since I was 15. When I get in high DRAG to perform, I add more makeup and hair, and amplify my female persona to an extreme level, so that I appear more like a DRAG queen."*

Not every performer derives all of his income from being a female impersonator. Most of them have regular jobs, dress as men.

"Female Impersonators are more than incredible performers and writers. They also, throughout their lives, hold great jobs"

Champagne T. Bordeaux (US Army Reserve), Stephanie Roberts (Local Public Service Company and before that the IRS), Kiki LaFlare Santangilo (911 Operator/Dispatcher, Freelance Photographer, Gay Activist), Selina Kyle (Barrista, Ice Rink Manager, Retail outlets,

Customer Service for AT&T), Lacey Lynn Taylors (Classical musician and play oboe and English horn with several ensembles as well as the Baroque oboe with a period instrument ensemble),

LaKeisha Pryce (worked for an Adult Rehabilitation Center for adults with mental disabilities), Nairobi V. D'Viante (Cutting counter at the fabric store), Wendel Duppert (Production Designer, coat check girl), Dee Gregory (Computer Systems Field Engineer, father of three).

Name the performers without checking on
DRAG411.com

"Does or did your job know
you performed as a female impersonator?"

Jocelyn Summers, *"Yes, I work at Hamburger Mary's in Tampa, Florida as a cook during the day and do the shows Saturday and Sunday nights. It is one of the greatest places to work, especially for the girls. On the staff right now (not show staff), we have one queen (me) and five transsexuals. I cannot think of another business ever to give the transsexual and DRAG community a safe loving environment to work in."*

Mystique Summers, *"My job loved me performing. When I quit to do the TV show, RuPaul's DRAG Race, they stopped work each week to watch.*

Cherry Darling, *"My day job knows I am a DRAG princess at night. DRAG queen sounds so very old and I simply don't have the crow's feet to be a DRAG queen. They love it when I relive tales of sordid shows and mischievous goings on."*

Jaeda Fuentes, *"My job when I lived in Michigan knew, but I was the boss there so it was never an issue. My regional manager did love my energy and the music I would always play in my retail store, so I think the DRAG helped."*

*Read the much larger, detailed, and updated
Book 8 of The Black Books,
The DRAG Queen Guide.*

**"I do not impersonate women.
How many women
do you know who march
around in 7-inch heels,
3-foot wigs and skin-tight outfits?"**
Rupaul

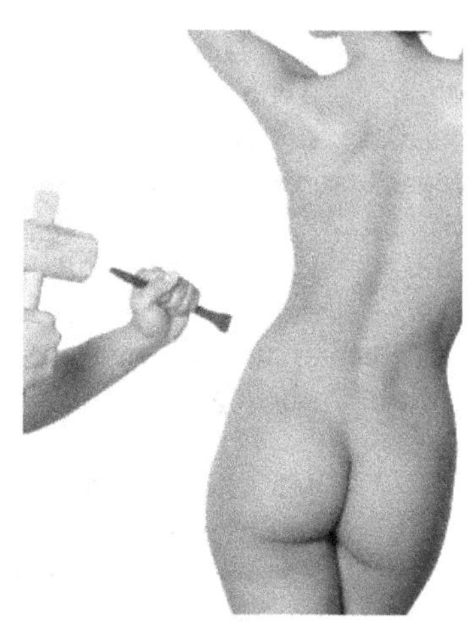

A rose by any other name is still Helen. The name a performer uses today is seldom the first name they acquired when entering the stage.

Only straight people in a bar believe a female impersonator's name is their first pet's name combined with the name of the street they grew up on as a child. Not one performer in this book listed the pet and street system for acquiring their current name. I am going to assume if you meet a performer acquiring their name in this manner, they were a drunk straight boy sitting on a tiled floor in a bar in Dayton, Ohio.

Naomi Wynters *(Divinity Tascha Fierce)*, Daphne Ferraro *(Kira LaVoy)*, Deva DaVyne *(Miss Deva Knight Summerz)*, Selina Kyle *(Miss Ginger Lace)*, Misty Eyez *(Reeka Shaye)*, Diamond Dunhill *(Meredith Monistat)*, BJ Stephens *(Maxine DelRio)*, Melissa Morgan, Amanda Love, *Felina Cashmere (Evita)*, Diedra Windsor Walker *(Ima Giho)*, Holly Berry *(Cherry Poppins)*, Kiki LaFlare Santangilo *(Kiki LaFlare)*, Adrian Leigh, Anatasia Fallon *(Anastasia Jynx Fallon)*, Pandora DeStrange *(Annastesia Burns)*, Shealita BaBay, Conundrum, Lisa Carr *(Miss Tori Novel)*, Lady Clover Honey, Stephanie Roberts *(Marlene Stevens)*, Barbra Herr *(Bobby Hernandez)*, Jade Shanell, Kori Stevens *(Kori Michaels)*, Ororo *(Erica Summers)*, Brianna Lee *(Bo-Vine)*, Kier Sarkesian *(Madame Suicide)*, Toni DaVyne *(Karmyn Bluntz)*, Jessica Jade, Tatum Michelle, Madisyn de la Mer *(Madisyn Dubai)*, Champagne T. Bordeaux *(Champagne Seville)*,

Mis Sadistic, Patricia Mason, Jocelyn Summers, Katrina Starr *(Layona Love)*, Wendy G. Kennedy *(Wendy Galento)*, Beverly LaSalle, Jade Jolie *(Jade Foxx)*, Jami Michaels *(Anita Dambeer)*, LeeAnna Love *(Cherri Bombb)*, Cartier Paris *(Dominique Devereaux)*, Dmentia Divinyl *(Eva LaDeva)*, Geraldine Queen Cabaret *(Geraldine)*, Brandi Marie, Alisa Summers, Santana Demonica Da Baum, Juwana Jackson, Esme Russell *(Nicole Torres)*, Crystal Belle *(Crystal Envy)*, *(Persia Azrael)*, Lacey Lynn Taylors, Eunyce Raye *(Jessyca Van Damme)*, Joey Brooks *(Lil General)*,

Glitz Glam *(Glitz)*, Afeelya Bunz, Teri Courtney, Nairobi V. D'Viante *(Nairobi)*, Echo Dazzle *(Cleo Torres)*, Phiore Liemont, Patricia Knight *(Passion)*, Babette Schwartz, Twat Sisters *(Ineeda Twat and Ima Twat)*, Vegas Platinum *(Chi Chi Ariola)*, Pussy LeHoot *(Topaz)*, Jade Daniels *(Jade)*, Rickie Lee, Raquel Payne, Monique Michaels, Jaeda Fuentes *(Jaeda Sky-Bankz)*, Dee Gregory, Angela Dodd, TotiYanah Diamond *(Precious Popular)*.

Since using pet names and street names are not how these performers decide on their names, this is how a majority of them actually obtained them:

- **Their DRAG mothers named them (37%)**
- **Their friends chose the name (36%)**
- **Named after someone famous (18%)**
- **They used a variation of their given name (5%)**
- **All other reasons (4%)**

Name the performers without checking on DRAG411.com

-

Not every name selection is viewed by the public with humor and adoration. Often, a female impersonator will select a name hinging on obscenity or use words often challenging the social norm. The Twat Sisters, Amanda Bone, Anita Cox, Pussy LaHoot, Maxi Pad.

(Following claims unverified by DRAG411)

Diamond Dunhill, *"Yes. The Dunhill Corporation warned me and my Webmaster to take down my website using the name Dunhill in the title. I became The #1 Search Engine on the internet For Dunhill Worldwide and they didn't like It. I was getting more hits than their sweater division or something! I had just started and it caused a stir. The site was terminated by my Webmaster."*

Champagne T. Bordeaux, *"Well, just folks always trying to buy champagne for me. I don't like it. I'm a Patron girl straight up, don't chill it, lime on side."*

Dmentia Divinyl, *"Well, Eva was controversial because I called her the Diva, which phonetically sounds like I'm Eva the Bitch, and as far as Dmentia, it is controversial whenever you choose a name that is a sad disease that people have as a chronic illness and can be a sad memory for people who deal with it in their personal life with themselves or others. I look at it this way, if you're not gonna laugh, you're gonna cry, either way, it's an emotional response and it makes people react, which is why I do entertainment in the first place. So be it."*

Pussy LeHoot, *"Oh my yes. Pussy – are you kidding me? I can't even use it on my facebook profile. What an injustice. It was never meant as anything sexual, it was chosen because of my "catlike' eyes, which have made many a men to do wrong over the years."*

BukkakeBlaque London St James, *"Use urban dictionary and please just look up my first name! Bukkake!"*

For the average female impersonator, controversy is NOT an external force from the straights in the community. They fight their greatest battle within the four walls of the venue that they selected to perform.

A performer rarely battles the stereotypes of customers that are not into DRAG and bar owners that believe they are owed special consideration. No group within those four walls is more vicious than the other female impersonators that share that dressing room. I tried very hard in this part of the book to not be vicious. I am standing here on my soapbox with my arms in the air, flowing back and forth singing "Can't we all just be friends?"

I planned to save anger for another chapter, aptly titled "Anger."

Chapter Three Images: First Image: Clare Bloomfield / FreeDigitalPhotos.net, Second Image: jscreationzs / FreeDigitalPhotos.net, Third Image: Salvatore Vuono / FreeDigitalPhotos.net, Fourth Image: Idea go / FreeDigitalPhotos.net, Fifth Image: Michal Marcol / FreeDigitalPhotos.net, Sixth Image: Idea go / FreeDigitalPhotos.net, Seventh Image: africa / FreeDigitalPhotos.net, Eighth Image: FreeDigitalPhotos.net.

Voted Top Three Books
I asked for the top three books
To help performers

Four books made the top three books, and they were all by the same author, Kevyn Acoin: Does not include DRAG411 Books since this was the first DRAG411 book.

- **Face Forward**,
  - Little, Brown. 2000. 175p. illus.
  - (# 0-316-28644-3., # 0-316-28705-9.)
- **Making Faces**,
  - Little, Brown. 1999. 160p. illus.
  - (# 0-316-28686-9., # 0-316-28685-0.)
  - *Tied with a split vote:*

The Art of Makeup,
- Harper-Collins Publishers. 1994. 176p. illus.
  - (# 0-060-17186-3.)
- **The Art of Makeup**,
- Perennial Currents. 1996. 176p. illus.
  - (# 0-062-73042-8.)

**Many impersonators create
their own stories, such as**

"Joey Brooks,
The Show Must Go On"

By Joey Brooks
With Todd Kachinski

Order your copy at DRAG411.com

"All sins are forgiven once you start making a lot of money."
RuPaul

❀ ❀ ❀

Chapter Four

Nobody Does It Better

Most parts of the country female impersonators create their own social networks to create support systems. This is not the same as a group finding you work. 99.87% of all female impersonators are left to themselves to find a gig. This has more to do with finding other female impersonators to socialize as a group. Some of the possible opportunities recommended by other performers include:

- **DRAG family**
- **Associates in the bar where they perform**
- **Fellow performers hang out together without a set structure, just common interest**
- **Imperial Court System functions as a fundraising entity**
- **DRAG It Out! teaches the art in South Florida**
- **Arizona Gender Outlaws or other groups operated by performers**

When you are a child in high school, you watch people struggling through life. You see classmates around you, each with their own crisis, battling their way through puberty. Thirty years will pass and those same teenagers will fondly remember their cherished days of adolescence. To be funny, this would imply life only goes downhill after age thirteen.

I am always amazed at all of my old school friends glorifying the 1980's, the years of disco, as if those were the best days of their lives. As once again, it adversely implies since 1980 everything in their life crumbled, which inspired me to ask the performers to define their memories of the early days. Some of these girls just became legal to drink, so for them; the early days could possibly be months ago.

Naomi Wynters, *"I remember my early days as something special, tragic, and fun. I say all these things because we all start out rough and we have to have the bad with the good. I was definitely tragic; I had no idea what I was doing with makeup at all. As a guy I wore only Chapstick. That was the extent of makeup for me. I wouldn't change any of those days."*

Deva DaVyne, *"Special and fun with a hint of tragic. Face it, each lady boy out there can't just throw on some Revlon lipstick and Bobby Brown eye shadow and walk out the house expecting to look FABULOUS! DRAG is fun and creative. We grow and learn, but it is also a disciplined art. The more you practice and perfect your techniques, the more people will be like 'Wow, she looks amazing' 'That girl can beat some face.'"*

Amanda Bone, *"It was a lot of trial and error and fun, lots of fun. But, it was lots of work."*

Amanda Love, *"No one has an easy time in the beginning. You really don't realize what you've gotten yourself into. Looking back I can laugh, though there were times I just wanted to hang it up."*

Champagne T. Bordeaux, *"My beginning days were tough. Back then there were a lot of girls coming out at the same time, so you had to be up on the game."*

Mis Sadistic, *"The beginning days were the best days of my life. The influences the girls had on me stayed with me all these years, funny when I started to write about them, it seems like just yesterday. When AIDS hit, I mean before they had a name for it, we started to lose people. That summer devastated the Fire Island community, so many passed, one by one. My friends, n   r to me than my own family."*

Lady Tajma Hall, *"The beginning days were so much fun. The early days taught*
me how to be a female impersonator, deal with show directors, present myself, how to enjoy the audience and how to deal with fellow entertainers. Those days were not easy but they were lots of fun. I would not change one thing about them."

Kori Stevens, *"OMG, those were the days. Those times taught me so much about what it really means to entertain, and even more importantly, about being me."*

Amy DeMilo, *"My beginning days were the best. It was the first time I ever felt like I fit in somewhere, applauded."*

Lady Clover Honey, *"The beginning was truly magical. I was discovering my true self and finding it wonderful to express myself that way. I felt like the ugly duckling when he first transformed into a swan."*

Beverly LaSalle, *"In the beginning, I didn't take my costuming too seriously. I thought I could just throw on a dress, some makeup and a wig, and get on stage. So, even though it was fun, I was still rough around the edges."*

Alisa Summers, *"Without the past, we can't get to the future. I have had a very fast and successful career so far. There have been situations that I could have done without, but without those experiences I wouldn't be who I am right now. My beginning days are a blessing."*

Jay Santana, *"Something incredible. So much to learn and so little time to really get ready!"*

Lacey Lynn Taylors, *"Looking back, those years were great fun, but highly tragic. Beginners always think they just look fantastic and perform even better, but when I think back, I was, as we say in the business, "a booger." Everyone has to start somewhere."*

Glitz Glam, *"Totally fun and tragic at the same time. For the first time I was able to express myself in a different way. Even though I was a hot mess, I was accepted for being different and I loved it!"*

Babette Schwartz, *"My DRAG birth was amazing! The lights, the music, the audience, all the stars aligned that night. Of course I looked a mess, but I* *didn't know any better and couldn't have cared less. I was having fun, darn it!"*

Jade Daniels, *"I definitely remember them as being special."*

Barbra Seville, *"the beginning was just fun. I used to be embarrassed to see my old pictures or routines, but now I look back fondly on being so innocent and wide eyed."*

Rickie Lee, *"Fun, scary, adventurous all at the same time."*

Vegas Platinum, *"It was all so new and exciting. It was quite a change from country life to the city and the wonder of it all. I had so much fun. I think I am still chasing that high I got off of doing DRAG in the beginning."*

At this point inside the book, the female impersonator has transitioned herself into the early version of the performer that she will someday be. This is also the point of the book where I separate those people placing their dress on to be transgender and those that wish to add performing to their resume. I determined that the focus of this book is female impersonators that perform, so at some point the decision is made to approach a venue. Only one male impersonator completed the survey (though through facebook hundreds were invited). I'm pretty sure most of them thought I was SPAM or ignored the message completely.

"Were you attending shows right from the beginning?"

Deva DaVyne, *"Yes, actually within four months. I was backstage helping other girls get ready. One girl didn't show up, so they looked at me and said, 'you're on'. Right after that I started getting paid bookings to work with some pretty amazing performers."*

Lady Sabrina, *"I had never seen a DRAG show until I was part of one. Probably added to the hot mess of it all, me doing what I think is sexy."*

BJ Stephens, *"I won a bunch of talent shows, so the owner decided it was cheaper to just hire me."*

Lady Tajma Hall, *"I attended shows before I started performing. I did not regularly attend, but I would try to go once a month. Eventually, I was going every week, sometimes twice a week."*

Kori Stevens, *"I competed in a talent show and won, which brought me to the Talent Show Finals. I won the finals and was hired onto a show cast immediately. I was so excited to be a working girl so fast, but I had no clothes!"* (Author's note: I found this comment entertaining after attending several fundraisers where all the performers seemed to be wearing clothes sewn by Kori Stevens)

Pandora DeStrange, *"I first got the DRAG bug after seeing The Rocky Horror Picture Show with a full shadow cast in Washington, DC. I was hooked!"*

Esme Russell, *"I've been doing shows since the Nina, Pinta and Santa Maria set sail for the New World. As I recall, I did a lot of entertaining once we arrived."*

How many performers in this book can you name without going to DRAG411.com?

Chapter Four Images: jscreationzs / FreeDigitalPhotos.net

❀❀❀
Chapter Five

Anger

If you are reading this chapter, I will be amazed, as no chapter in this book had as much trouble finding inclusion. If I would have been smart (which I am not) I would have typed out this chapter to get it off my chest, threw it in the garbage can, and moved on.

My relationship with the Florida gay bar community is quite extensive. As a young man, I watched my very first female impersonator, Joey Brooks, dance across the stage to the tune "Turn Around Bright Eyes." I write graphically violent crime novels, and in Turn Around, a serial killer is crossing the country killing female impersonators.

In the novel, one of the characters is a Latin female impersonator brutally murdered in Phoenix forcing the country to deal with hate crimes against performers.

I have never dated a female impersonator. I have never, as an adult, put on a dress. Not a single person in my inner circle of friends was active as a female impersonator around me. Do not get me wrong, of the 2,714 female impersonators involved in this project, I now know half of them. Of the 1,200 I know, at least 400 of them have shared experiences with projects in my life. Of the 400 performers, less than a dozen I speak to on a weekly basis. Of the twelve people I spoke to, (mostly on facebook) only three were truly active friends in my life. Of the three active friends in my life, zero I speak to on the phone on a monthly basis.

Pause and look at the paragraph I just wrote. If there was anyone less qualified to write this book, I would be surprised. "Turn Around Bright Eyes" needed Cassandra to be the richest character of my new novel. I had no resource information at my disposal to create this incredible person.

I started college for theatrical arts, because I wanted to be a playwright. I knew enough about stage to realize information I would get off the internet regarding makeup would be false for my character. I believe I have the most creative imagination of any person I have ever met in my life; on the verge of insanity, but it is okay, I find it entertaining.

I was given the opportunity through twenty-two facebook accounts to reach out to a couple friends to ask for their insight. I decided to set up a facebook group, post the questions, and beg profusely for their attention. It was my desire, originally, my DRAG friends would come to my rescue, so I could write my next best-selling book.

My facebook posts caught the attention of an entire nation of female impersonators assuming I was writing "literally a book about them." After receiving a quarter of a million words, I realized "Turn Around Bright

Eyes" would have to be set aside. From 2010 to 2015, I completed over two dozen books.

Those books were "My Books." By the time I pulled the questions down from facebook I realized, the next project no longer belonged to me. It belonged to the 2,714 female impersonators interacting in the largest GLBTQ project of this nature in history. One of my interns laughed, realizing unexpectedly, I had become "The DRAG Whisperer."

This book is not "My Book." This book became their book. It literally overnight became "The Original, Official DRAG Handbook." It was like buying a compact vehicle online and showing up at the car lot to find you just purchased The Partridge Family bus.

One of the projects my publishing group was considering involved a local photographer. A few days later, the photographer and I had met for lunch in Ybor City, Tampa, Florida. As we sat there in the cafe discussing his photo project, we stumbled across the word "DRAG." We discussed if mutual friends would avoid contributing to the book because I adopted "DRAG" in the new book title.

I went home after lunch and posted online for entertainers to give me their viewpoints on the title. They shared hundreds of opinions, but the part catching me off guard was not the anger coming from the people against the word, but the performers against the female impersonators not liking the word. The conversation was not constructive and extremely mean spirited. Post after post belittled the performers having a problem with the word.

DRAG has been around since Shakespeare. Its origin, contrary to belief, is unknown. In the late 1500's, the English terminology denoted a Boy

DRessed **A**s a **G**irl. It was a footnote placed on a script to denote the attire of a character. It was not a slang created out of anger, hate, or social repression. As I read the dictionary explanations across a dozen web sites, I realized the origin of this word best described this project. This book, once again I repeat, is not marketed to transgender people. Its newly defined focus was on male entertainers **DR**essed **A**s a **G**irl for the purpose of "entertainment."

I personally know many performers refused to be in this book because it used the word DRAG. They personally sent me letters. They explained they did not want to be in the book, because they were transgender or transsexual performers. Nothing hateful. Nothing mean spirited. I would like to believe this project done by me is my proof I have an open mind for open debate.

Name the performers without checking on DRAG411.com

Opposing opinions are shared equally in this book's contents. I applaud people having convictions to stand up for their beliefs. The only problem I had with performers refusing to become part of this project, based on the word DRAG, were 92% of them were performing on a monthly basis in events billed as "DRAG shows." A person with true conviction on a marquis, for an event at a bar, that allows the venue's bartenders to confirm to inquiring customers of an impending DRAG show, confuse me.

The same passion used for removing themselves from this book should equally apply to every single bar allowing their staff or customers to use the word DRAG. Many of these performers were able to compromise their values based on a paycheck.

There is a reason they call stereotypes - stereotypes. I was hoping to crush my largest stereotype for female impersonators by my research. I wanted to believe secretly the performers showed love and adoration on stage behaved accordingly in the dressing room. I was proven wrong.

I do not have a psychology degree. I'm not going to pretend to understand why so much negative energy is packed inside such a small space behind the stage. I am not going to pretend watching RuPaul's shows gives me the understanding of why these performers go out of their way to be so mean spirited. I was told by several of the RuPaul performers, their "airtime was based on drama." I'm sure cocktails helped too. I once created a quote,

**"Placing LOL after a mean comment does not make
the comment funny. It makes you an ass."**
Todd Kachinski Kottmeier

We do not accept public humiliation at a regular job, so why do we accept it in a social setting?

If their conviction is this makes them honest, this means they walk through the stores randomly stopping people to totally humiliate and tear them down for the sake of honesty. For some reason, many (notice I did not say most) performers feel it is their duty to shred other people's lives in an attempt to elevate their own. As a child, many of us are taught you do not become a bigger person by tearing everyone else around you down. You become a better person when you reach out with compassion to offer guidance.

The, "Oh no girl, you didn't" response performers seek, is not a true alternative to true wit. Fortunately, there are hundreds of performers, which lead their lives with their heart. They are the mentors reaching out to hold their hand, to hug them when they cry, to share in their laughter, to motivate and to inspire. Very few performers "in action" seek to be this person, and it is sad. Those people will transform their art.

The most bizarre emails came from fifty-four performers across the country stating they did not want to be in the book because someone they disliked was in the book. As a teacher, I find this very confusing, but I blame myself, because I do not teach third grade.

"Doing what I do for a living has never been easy. I've had to fight
countless battles in this game
that the public has no idea ever happened.
I just pick myself up and carry on, I carry on."
RuPaul

Throughout the questionnaire's sampling, I often wondered what the ratios were of letters sent in compared to those who did not respond (but shared the same belief). Even if it was 4 to 1, which any business owner will tell you the number is closer to 10 to 1, would imply that hundreds of performers refused to be in the project because another performer was in it. It inspired me to ask the participants how drama was handled in the venues.

Jocelyn Summers, *"Well that is just ridiculous. We have a hard enough time being who we are in this world and to have people in the same place in life bring each other down is just silly. People need to just worry about themselves and move on."*

Jade Shanell, *"It's bad enough we get hate from the world from people that don't understand us but to get hate from fellow gay men and queens is just a shame."*

Ororo, *"Drama is going to go on wherever you are. Just be yourself and let your light shine."*

Fallon, *"Generally venues themselves don't really get involved. I think it is a big mistake to allow drama behind the scenes. Just like any job, you may have to work with people you don't particularly care for. As a professional, it is your duty to make it work for the sake of the show."*

Allure, *"I have booked people that don't get along with each other several times. I let them know in advance that we will not deal with any drama."*

Beverly LaSalle, *"I have had various performers tell venues that they will not work there because I was there. Most of the time, I was the one that took the stage. I have no tolerance for drama, and if someone won't perform with me, that is their issue, not mine or the venue's."*

Adora, *"I think jealousy is a waste of time. We all have different talents and it's all up to the audience. When I go to work, I go to work."*

Part of the bitterness I encountered comes from the young entertainers viewing the older performers as scary dinosaurs. It is easy to forget the path of their success and opportunities were earned on the sweat of the person they tear

down. A few of the younger performers will latch on to an experienced female impersonator they designate as their DRAG mother.

Too many times the respect many of them share for the pioneers of their craft is superficial and mean spirited. For every entertainer remaining on the stage, two decades later, represents thousands of female impersonators that have left the art.

Jocelyn Summers, *"I have taken a little bit of every entertainer I have ever watched and have been advised by. Whether good or bad I took the information and decided to go on my own path. As the saying goes," It takes a village..."*

Kori Stevens, *"Nobody is an island. Whether people are for you or against you, they help make you who you are, it's that simple."*

Mr. Kenneth Baker, *"If it weren't for the support of the audiences and the other entertainers we encounter and learn from along the way, we would still be stuck lip-synching to a Diana Ross record in our bathroom mirror, with a towel on our head and a hairbrush in our hand."*

Anastasia Rexia, *"I don't care if people say they have not been helped. We have ALL been helped either directly or indirectly. We are influenced and take the trailblazers for granted. There are people out there who opened doors for you."*

Wendell Duppert, *"It's all in your approach and attitude. I've found an amazing community of talented, caring gay men. If you're only "in it to win it" you're going to be pretty lonely. If you're enjoying the journey, and are a little less self-centered and a little more giving, all of the right people will come into your life."*

Jade Daniels, *"I'm a firm believer in doing unto others as you would have others do unto you. So, if you feel everyone was against you, maybe you did something to deserve it."*

Lola Honey, *"Nobody can give you your talent, creativity, or drive. We all have had someone that put an opportunity in front of us to make us prosper. Without these foot-in-the-door opportunities, I don't think any entertainer would be where they are."*

Shugah Caine, *"I have many friends and loved ones who have supported Shugah. I have also found that many folks will smile in your face as they stab you in the back.. Not all, but we know the bitchy queens are out there."*

Tiffani Middlesexx, *"I have been so fortunate in my career as well as in my life to have been encouraged and sometimes financially aided in my quest to be the best. It has changed so much over the years, and not always for the better."*

Katrina Starr, *"Everyone I have met has helped me in some way or another. Those who had bad things to say or a negative attitude to me or my craft made my skin thicker and prepared me for the future, because I'm sure I'll face worse people and attitudes in my years to come."*

Kori Stevens, *"I've been there to see a line-up changed so a certain person could perform a song before someone else."*

Selina Kyle, *"The funniest I have seen involved two performers. Both had locking dressing rooms, and they both used a regular keyed padlock. One got upset at the other and poured super glue in the other's padlock. It wasn't a difficult fix, but it took a while for the owners to get there with bolt cutters so that he could start getting ready."*

Beverly LaSalle, *"I think one of the funniest things I have ever seen was a fellow performer walking around the hotel in Miami, Florida, after the Miss Florida Pageant, in nothing but tits and makeup."*

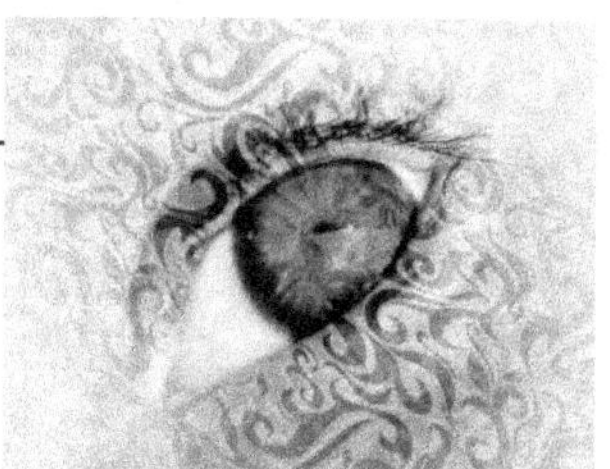

Cartier Paris, *"One girl who decided to perform the same song I performed, on the same night, fell off the stage during her performance."*

Jay Santana, *"At the Warehouse in Cedar Rapids, Iowa, one of the girls had some horrid handwriting. The MC announced her as Dessert Tray...her name...Desiree."*

Lacey Lynn Taylors, *"I was performing one night at a club and started to get ready. I had used an old beaded gown and cut it up to use the parts for a "showgirl" costume. I had just put it on when one of the other entertainers says 'Bitch, that's my gown!' I had, unbeknownst to me, been given a stolen gown from another queen and had used it to make my costume."*

Eunyce Raye, *"I had another fat queen tell me that I needed to lose weight."*

The definition of honesty has been debated for as long as man has stood upright. I don't necessarily know if being obnoxiously aggressive defines a person as being honest. To tell the truth, I do not believe most of the remarks come from a place in the person's heart, but under the false belief, it makes them witty.

Taking the leap into the dressing room takes thick skin, sometimes a jaded belief system, and a false hope, believing dry wit is a substitution for honesty. A fresh female impersonator may prefer not to take this journey alone.

Daphne Ferraro, *"Definitely bring a friend along. One thing I learned about queens is that they are brutally honest"*

Felina Cashmere, *"I started out by myself, but along the way I met my DRAG sister, Nairobi D'Viante, and we sharde everything together in terms of DRAG. I inspired two others, which are now my DRAG daughters. I never thought or meant to inspire others to do DRAG, it just happened. I love that fact."*

Kenya, *"My husband is there with me through it all. I also shop with one of the greatest queens in the area."*

Naomi D'Lish, *"I always bring a straight girlfriend. I'm sorry, but they are women and they are blunt and real, so why shouldn't we listen to their input?"*

Rhyana Vorhman, *"I was taught by my boss and many other queens. They taught me the tricks of the trade, and that we must stop fighting among ourselves and help each other. When a new queen wants to learn the business, I will always help them. They are the ones that will continue the tradition long after we are gone."*

Some of those early bonds create partnerships which become an integral part of the act. Ineeda and Ima Twat from the very first day became a comedy act. We asked many of the performers if they had a sister in arms, a partner in crime the Ying to their Yang.

Many of the best DRAG duos include: *Ima and Ineeda Twat (The Twat Sisters), Lola Honey and Samorah Honey, Miss Gigi and Kimmie Parker, Amanda Love and Chanel Chevonne, Selina Kyle and Ifeelya Cummings, Wendy G. Kennedy and Monica Synclair, Jami Michaels and Monica Jeffries, Patricia Mason and Eryka Knowles, PurrZsa Kyttyn and Alexiya St Martin, Shae Shae LaReese and Marisa K. Devine, Rickie Lee and Dee Gregory, Jaeda Fuentes and CoCo Montrese, Jade Daniels and Nicole Paige Brooks.*

Most of the female impersonators viewed the more experienced performers in an extremely hostile manner. Along the way, generation after generation of performers has taught each other to disrespect the generation before them while placing a superficial face of affection. It overwhelms me on the amount of negative letters secretly poured into my office slamming performers only 15 to 20 years older than themselves. I was puzzled watching each of them publicly post, in adoration, their DRAG mother, and the other elders on stage, as an influence on their career. The profession will never reach its deserved potential as long as the people disrespect it the most are the people are in the middle of it all.

Respect is the obligation of every female impersonator. Changing the sour comments overwhelming the dressing room will not change overnight, as too many people, for far too long, have made it acceptable behavior. It is the personal obligation of those people, which designate themselves as DRAG mothers, to insure the behavior starts today. In real life, our mothers taught us, it is inappropriate to piss on the dining room table while we are eating.

Common sense is ONLY something someone taught us. Changing bad behavior is going to have to start at the top. Thousands of female impersonators across the country are designated as DRAG mothers. Hundreds of them replied, "they had so many DRAG children; they could not possibly list them all." Starting today, they should have a moral obligation for the behavior of every single person holding them up for respect.

DRAG411's DRAG Memorial page on DRAG411.com

Also "REST IN PEACE" these two DRAG411 Volunteers

Kyle Taplin typed in the first name to the DRAG411 database, and continued to type until he could type no more. Today the database created, is the largest organization of male and female impersonators in GLBT history.

Kim Perkins mentored 62 DRAG411 facebook pages and groups, with almost 2.7 million fans and readers. Other than Steve Hammond and myself, Kim Perkins was the only person on earth to read every comment sent in for all of those groups and the dozens of books created from their content.

Photos in Chapter Five: First Image: Idea go / FreeDigitalPhotos.net, Second Image: Filomena Scalise / FreeDigitalPhotos.net, Third Image: Salvatore Vuono / FreeDigitalPhotos.net Fourth Image: Rawich / FreeDigitalPhotos.net, Fifth Image: Filomena Scalise / FreeDigitalPhotos.net, Sixth Image: Filomena Scalise / FreeDigitalPhotos.net, Seventh Image: renjith krishnan / FreeDigitalPhotos.net, Eighth Image: Idea go / FreeDigitalPhotos.net, Nineth Image: Filomena Scalise / FreeDigitalPhotos.net, Tenth Image: Daniel St.Pierre / FreeDigitalPhotos.net

Chapter Six

Makeup

❀ ❀ ❀

Nothing is sadder than
 watching a performer enter the stage
a scary mess. Probably the only thing
worse would be the entertainer
enters the stage as a pretty girl and
leaves as a scary man.

**"Explain your rules
about facial makeup?"**

Naomi Wynters, *"Cover Girl doesn't cover
boys. In DRAG... more is always better."*

Anastasia Fallon, *"The one thing I can no
longer do without is my Ben Nye powder.
It's simply amazing and lasts forever."*

Mis Sadistic, *"For my facial makeup
I start with my cheeks, contouring them with
a darker color. I never go above the cheekbone,
so it creates a check mark under the cheek to the
hairline on an upward angle. Over the cheek,
I add press powder up to the lower lash line,
and that gives the illusion of a larger cheek.
I use the least expensive makeup I can
find, since I find the result to be the same.
I use powders from Big Lots, CVS, Walgreen's."*

Selina Kyle, *"Just some general guidelines: For most of us Coty powder is the
best for your foundation, some apply it with a powder puff and others apply
it with a powder brush, it's up to your personal preference. My advice is that
for shading you want a sharp edge to help redefine your face. I use a piece
of cardboard held flat against my face to get an amazing new facial structure
to work with. For highlighting, I use Ben Nye's Super White face powder. For
blush, I use three colors ranging from darkest to lightest. Always, always,
always clean your brushes after using them, it keeps them in good shape,*

and you want them to be the best they can be. You can find really good recipes for cleaner on YouTube along with how to use them."

Esme Russell, *"If you don't know what you're doing, seek a professional DRAG queen."*

PurrZsa Kyttyn, *"Mehron! And don't be afraid to let someone else paint you sometimes, you'll learn amazing tricks."*

Lacey Lynn Taylors, *"Some like La Femme, others like Ben Nye, but I only use MAC cosmetics. They simply work best for me. I use a combination of colors to achieve the desired shade. I also prefer very harsh lines for my contour and employ the use of a card with a straight edge. If you are a beginner, seek advice or use trial and error. Look at pictures of your favorite entertainers and try to mimic their look."*

Monique Michaels, *"I use either theatrical (Ben Nye, Kryolan) or MAC products. Contour with two colors for a smooth blend and two blush colors for a smoother air brushed look. I always contour the forehead, cheekbones and jaw line to make the face pop, but make sure you blend, no lines!"*

"Do you have (or did you have) a problem with acne?"

Lacey Lynn Taylors, *"Use a good facial cleanser and water to remove makeup. Moisturize heavily before painting and again after taking it off."*

Kiki LaFlare Santangilo, *"My hair stylist introduced me to the Rodan & Fields line of facial products, they work amazingly well. They have products for tons of different facial problems. They are a little expensive, but they work great. Once the acne cleared up, I switched to anti-aging products. I've always been told to start using anti-aging products BEFORE you actually need them. It's useless to start using anti-aging products at age 50, the face will already be drooping and those crow's feet will be walking all over your eyes."*

Anastasia Fallon, *"On occasion. The best trick I've learned is olive oil. It's good for non-oily skin, inexpensive, and it takes away the makeup the best I've seen in years."*

Selina Kyle, *"I try to give myself a nice spa day once in a while. Steam, scrub, exfoliate, masque to shrink pores. It makes my face feel wonderful."*

Lisa Carr, *"Sedona Spa has a fabulous Mineral Facial that is better than getting a facial at a spa. It's inexpensive and only takes about 20 minutes to suck all the junk out of pores, and even skin tone. It can even be applied in small sections over night for spot treatments of blemishes."*

Esme Russell, *"If you have acne, go to a dermatologist. Do not pick your pimples or squeeze them, it will scar your face. I've always had mild acne, but I've always used good products to treat it. My facial products are from Nova Cosmetics. Always remove your makeup."*

TotiYanah Diamond, *"I do have bad acne. It's best to go see a dermatologist. I recommend applying a moisturizer before applying makeup."*

"Explain your rules about facial foundation"

Diedra Windsor Walker, *"I used to love Pan Stick. I'm not sure how many other girls started out on that. Now when one finds a Pan Stick, it's like a Faberge Egg for our world. Since then, I have used various products from the Sephora store, but I miss my Pan Stick."*

Ryhana Vorhman, *"I use Dermablend. To make it thinner for application, I use a lighter to warm it up and make it liquefy and apply it with a sponge by dabbing it in. Set it with Dermablend All Cover powder."*

Jocelyn Summers, *"Facial Foundations, NO liquids, period! Lights make us sweat and liquids run; not cute!"*

Jade Shanell, *"I use NYX or Ben Nye makeup so it is highly pigmented so it canbe seen from the stage. Highlighting the face and shadowing is so important, and blend, blend blend."*

Lady Tajma Hall, *"MAC is my foundation of choice, but I use Kryolan on occasion. I found that rubbing a little Vaseline on my fingers gives the most even coverage and helps it spread easier."*

Brianna Lee, *"My foundation preference is DermaBlend I purchase from J C Penney or Dillard's. It fills blemishes and scarring. I heat the product with a blow dryer or zap it in a microwave for 10 seconds to make it go on smoothly and it lasts a lot longer. It also works well for shadowing the cheeks before you powder down."*

Lisa Carr, *"Most retail brands do not work well for DRAG queens. Pro entertainers almost always use theatrical or specialized lines like DermaBlend, Kryolan or Ben Nye."*

Anastasia Rexia, *"Kryolan TV Panstick is flawless and cheap. I don't think DermaBlend is worth the money."*

"Explain your rules about eye liner, shadows, makeup...?"

Amanda Love, *"MAC or LaFemme are great products that have wonderful pigmentation. Honey, start hanging out with DRAG queens, dressing them and watch them closely. Just practice practice practice until you get the eyes you love and that will be "your" eye."*

Jocelyn Summers, *"The more black around the eye, the more the eye will pop. It doesn't matter what other colors you choose to blend into it. I have also found that different colors make different eyes pop."*

Kori Stevens, *"My brand of choice for shadows and blushes is LaFemme. I think it is comparable to MAC but much less expensive. It goes on easily and the pigment is great. The tricks of applying is different for each person, but a general rule I use is if you are painting a smoky eye, use black to line and contour top and bottom. Use a lighter color on the lid and an even lighter color on the brow bone. It always works for me, and I have painted a LOT of people."*

Naomi D-Lish, *"My rule of thumb with shadows and liners is to invest in a good eye shadow primer and use it every time. You'll notice a difference if you don't"*

Ginger Minj, *"I am known for not being "afraid of the paint!" I will wear every color in my makeup case if given enough time. I have two palettes, one full of LaFemme blushes/bronzers/shadows and another full of Kryolan and Ben Nye."*

Glitz Glam, *"I would say try them all and see what works for you. Product is only half of it, skill is the rest. Glamor can't be bought, it must be taught!"*

Jaeda Fuentes, *"Use brands such as Mehron and Ben Nye, they work amazingly!"*

"Explain your rules about lipstick and other lip products?"

Lady Tajma Hall, *"I use MAC liner, lipstick, gloss and concealer. I first put Vaseline on my lips followed by alight application of concealer. I then line my lips with a MAC Currant lip liner followed by a light application of apricot lipstick. I then heavily brush with gold lip gloss for the look I love."*

Jade Jolie, *"I basically outline my lips for strong definition and color the corners. Follow that with a darker neutral lipstick and cover with a bright gloss or lip glass. Then use a small amount of the lightest pan stick for the lower center lip, and use Sally Hensen's Lip Plumper to finalize it all."*

Vegas Platinum, *"Don't line your lips in black unless you are blending heavily or doing a super dark lip. Lightest colors on the inside middle of the lip and darker as you work your way out."*

"What is the most effective way to remove makeup?"

Misty Eyez, *"Dish soap"*

Madisyn de la Mer, *"Ponds Cold Cream"*

Joey Brooks, *"Baby oil, then a wet one"*

Melissa Morgan, *"Soap and water, baby oil"*

Pandora DeStrange, *"MAC wipes"*

Makayla Rose Devine, *"Shampoo that has a conditioner mixed in"*

Leigh Shannon, *"Albolene, hands down"*

Nairobi V. D'Viante, *"Hot water and a facial scrub"*

Barbra Seville, *"Lavender baby oil"*

"Explain your rules about women's perfumes"

Melissa Morgan, *"I love Beyond Paradise, that's great."*

Adrian Leigh, *"Body spray – Vanilla or Cucumber/Melon"*
Alexis De La Mer, *"Cheap perfume lasts the whole night, but I love Chanel"*

Horchata, *"Ed Hardy Tattoo, the imitation. Sometimes body sprays."*

Tiffani Middlesexx, *"Red by Giorgio"*

Vivika D'Angelo, *"I just use body spray when I am performing, If I wear perfume to go to a club, I use Chanel"*

Juwana Jackson, *"My favorite is Red Pearl. It's inexpensive and smells rich"*

Babette Schwartz, *"I prefer Hawaiian Ginger, first the cologne, then the body spray. It is fresh, clean, and cheap. Like me!"*

"How do you get makeup out of your clothes?"

Amy DeMilo, *"Sometimes I use Goo Gone on fabrics that have gotten makeup or duct tape residue on them. Worst case scenarios, if you can't get a stain out, embellish it – add feathers, stones, etc to cover it up."*

Madisyn de la Mer, *"Goo Gone. Shout is awesome, and of course bleach for whites...and a lot of cursing!"*

Teri Courtney, *"Oxyclean makes a gel I swear by. I have gotten makeup and even chocolate stains out of sweaters"*

**"It is all of
our fault,
if we let
people tear each
other apart.**

**Respect cannot
survive in a
room of apathy."**

Todd Kachinski Kottmeier

*A fun book signing at Twist
in South Beach, Miami with
Hector Acevedo (above)
driving me from one tour stop
to the next.*

*John Behr (left)
assisting the efforts of
DRAG411'S project in
Sarasota, Florida. Food
dropped locally stayed locally.*

Chapter Six Photos: First Image: Suat Eman / FreeDigitalPhotos.net, Second Image: Rasmus
Thomsen / FreeDigitalPhotos.net

Chapter Seven

Shaving

❀ ❀ ❀

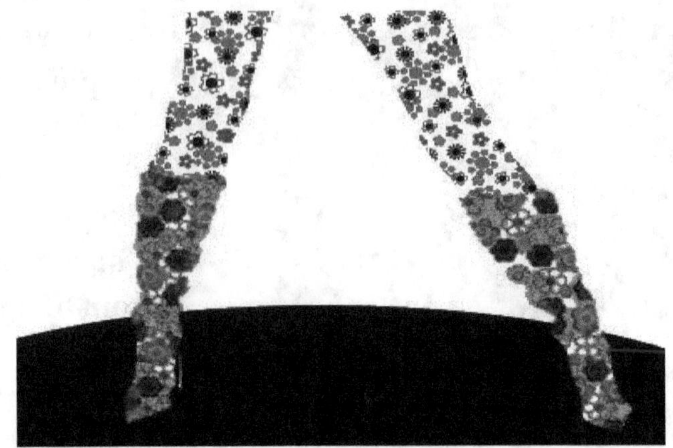

Talking on the phone with Ima Twat, reminded me of the vast differences of shaving legs. I just assumed every DRAG queen put the same shaving cream, they applied to their face, onto their legs, and grabbed a razor blade. Ima Twat explained that she was fortunate enough to be one of those hairless men that were able to use Nair to remove any random growth.

Ima let it be known that he hit strategic spots. It was funny that Ima found humor in the fact that her performing sister Ineeda Twat refused to shave her legs and proceeded to wear four layers of pantyhose.

"Explain your rules about shaving your legs"

Naomi Wynters, *"I don't shave my legs. I wear dance tights/panty hose to help with the illusion, as well as hide the hair on my legs and keep my hip padding in place."*

Tatum Michelle, *"I trim my leg hair with clippers and I just wear two pairs of pantyhose and a pair of tights."*

Barbra Herr, *"I don't shave, hormones took away the body hair, and there wasn't much anyway. I had electrolysis done on my face."*

Alisa Summers, *"I do not shave my legs, and I am a hairy boy! I wear two to three pairs of full coverage tights and it camouflages the hair."*

"Explain your rules about shaving your chest, arms and back."

Coco Labelle, *"Based on experience, multiple layers are your best bet without shaving, with exception of wearing open toed shoes. Three pairs of black footless tights will do the trick. Shaving can be tedious, but is worth it. I suggest Satin Care Sensitive shaving cream."*

Lady Tajma Hall, *"I suggest using laser for any parts of your upper body that are hairy. I Nair my legs once a week and it allows me to feel silky smooth at all times. Remember to moisturize your entire body, because that will make it easier on your skin."*

Ginger Minj, *"I have extremely sensitive skin. I have found that the only hair remover that works on me without burning my skin is the pink bottle of Sally Hansen's Hair Remover (available at Wal-Mart). It's heavy enough to remove my "winter coat", but sensitive enough that I can still shave problem spots without irritating my skin and breaking out."*

Jade Jolie, *"I love my Venus razor. No tricks, it's self-explanatory I think. Just moisturize and soften your hair. I do have an automatic razor for my arms."*

"Explain your rules about facial stubble"

Champagne T. Bordeaux, *"Well, I tried laser and that mess hurts! My goodness, why, why, why? Who came up with that torture? So, I use Strawberry sensitive shaving cream for ladies."*

Jade Daniels, *"Bearded ladies only work in the circus. I use Schick or Gillette with multiple blades but no cut guard wires over the blades. And, the one thing I cannot live without is my shaving oil from The Art of Shaving, it will save your face!"*

Diedra Windsor Walker, *"I constantly am fighting stubble, as hair grows fast on me. I do all I can to shave and shave to make sure I have a clear and smooth face."*

Anastasia Fallon, *"As I've gotten older, I find that a great razor with at least 3 blades. It has to be a smooth shave every time. Once upon a time, in my late teens/early twenties, I could use cheap disposable razors and go against the growth. I'd even dry shave or cold water shave when necessary. My skin will not take that abuse now that my hair has gotten a bit coarser."*

Name the performers without checking on DRAG411.com

Chapter 7 Photos: First Image: Salvatore Vuono / FreeDigitalPhotos.net, Second Image: graur razvan ionut / FreeDigitalPhotos.net, Image: graur razvan ionut / FreeDigitalPhotos.net

Chapter Eight

T!TS & @SS

The musical Chorus Line reminds us that it's all about t!ts and @ss. Placing your gym socks inside a bra doesn't cut it when you're in the limelight of a venue The audience of old school DRAG has become more sophisticated in the era of "Jurassic Park" technology.

Coco Labelle, *"The Marilyn Monroe brand Lingerie company makes a great butt pad in many sizes and goes on like underwear, highly padded, and costs about $15"*

Mis Sadistic, *"If you choose padding, you can use silicone prosthetics. These are very similar to the breast forms. They are held in place by a garment like a support pantie. You can find both items at Fredericks of Hollywood."*

Beverly LaSalle, *"Between the panty hose and the tight spandex costumes, I get all the lift I need...Thankfully!!!"*

Lacey Lynn Taylors, *"You can create hips with foam padding from a craft store, or mattress foam from most department stores. Use at least 1" thick, and cut two large pear shaped pads determining the length from the top of the knee to above the hipbone. Place two smaller similarly shaped pads beneath those for fullness, and one large oval pad for the back, with another smaller oval shaped pad underneath for fullness. Electric knives are used to bevel the edges and give a smooth appearance and thick dancer's tights are used to hold them in place."*

"Explain your rules about selecting your fake breasts size."

Kiki LaFlare Santangilo, " *BOOBIES! A lot of girls I perform with use random things to stuff with, foam, rubber, socks, etc. I however, use balloons. I get a lot of crap from the girls about that, but I feel it gives the most realistic look and feel. I would NOT suggest using water balloons, however. You wouldn't want to pop a titty on stage and shower your audience. I'm a plus size girl, so I actually lift my "man-boobs" and place my balloons under them. My bra is padded so when I put it on it creates the look of an actual boob, instead of a lumpy implant. Make sure you always carry a few extra balloons with you in your kit just in case one pops or gets a hole in it. I normally purchase white or clear party balloons at Party City and they will last for quite a while. I can blow up and use one pair for several weekends before I'll throw them away and make more. Bigger girls need bigger breasts and smaller girls need smaller ones. Breasts that match your chest size just look more natural"*

BJ Stephens, *"I use a mixture of foam shoulder pads and homemade pouches of foam filling. I'm a 40DD, big girl, big boobs!"*

Jocelyn Summers, *"Nerf is a girl's best friend. One $3.00 ball and you have two boobies!"*

Anastasia Rexia, *"I first made my hips and then slowly made the split pea boobs (end of a nylon using split peas) fill them up one half cup at a time until they look right, then tied them off and measured."*

"Explain your rules about selecting your breast size (Implants)"

Melissa Morgan, *"Each person is different, I want to do America System, so I can't have them. Also, I chose to be an all boy queen."*

Lady Tajma Hall, *"Please allow your doctor to guide you. The doctor can tell you what size best suits your body and what size will settle well in your body. You want your breasts to look natural, not like a freak show."*

Amy DeMilo, *"I got implants as a job enhancement, never to be a woman, only to emulate. I had one size picked out and on my way to the operating table I saw pictures on the wall and said 'that's what I want.' That's what I got, and couldn't be happier.*

Chapter Eight Photos: First Image: Salvatore Vuono / FreeDigitalPhotos.net

Name the performers without checking on
DRAG411.com

Chapter Nine

Wigs

❀ ❀ ❀

When I asked this question, I made the mistake of posting a copy and paste of wig dimensions and sizes for the performers to use as a reference guide. I was under the false impression that female impersonators selected their wigs using the same criteria. Boy was I wrong. On average, the participants stated that they purchased their first wig when they were eighteen years old and 91.2% purchased a wig with elastic. If it fits, wear it.

Maxine Padlock, *"Twenty-three inches and they all have elastic."*

Rhyana Vorhman, *"All of my wigs have elastic in them."*

Selina Kyle, *"I am definitely a large, but all of my wigs usually have an elastic band or two, and if I'm dancing, that wig will be pinned, tied, and usually weave bonded down to my head. I don't like wigs coming off in the middle of splits, cartwheels, round-offs or other acrobatics."*

Amanda Bone, *"I've never measured, I just grab and go."*

"Explain your rules about using wigs"

Misty Eyez, *"My rule for wigs, NEVER use just one. Any brand, any color, any style, it's all a matter of taste. I buy them at small little ghetto stores to big suppliers in Miami. Favorite wig store is in Chicago. I think it is called Heads N Threads."*

Esme Russell, *"Wigs are bought on personal taste. I have 20 or more wig stores I shop at, some online. Wig America online is great. Every city has wig stores that can help you. My favorite wig lines are Rene of Paris (very high end), Allure (middle of the road) and Wig America (the Wal-Mart of wig lines)."*

Diedre Windsor Walker, *"Yes, the hair. I like Glamour Puss, as that is the brand My Mama uses and I like how I look in them. But, Texas hair baby, go big or go home. If I wear a gown, I prefer up do and lace front wigs have been what I have used."*

"Explain your rules about using your real hair"

Mis Sadistic, *"When I use my real hair, I blend it with a piece. If I use a piece and gel it down to add falls, buns and ponytails, I attach the pieces so they look believable over and around my hair. The trick is to blend your own hair with the piece."*

Brianna Lee, *"I always use my hair to blend into the front and or side of a wig that matches and is not a character wig. When I do characters such as Lucy or Divine, I have to hide my own hair completely."*

Miss Gigi, *"My real hair...what little I have I hide under my wigs."*

Alisa Summers, *" I use my real hair only as a base to hold on wigs and pieces. I find that wigs are easier to work with than natural hair."*

"Do you often just use your own hair or tend to use a wig?"

Misty Eyez, *"I've blended in my own hairline, but I've never done DRAG without a wig"*

Jocelyn Summers, *"A combination of both is best. You need something to add volume and length for a more dramatic stage presence. Using your own hair in adds more realism. Pull your own hair up and add a ponytail, or just adding your bangs to the front provides a much more natural look."*

Dmentia Divinyl, *"I'm bald now, so I must use wigs. I do have an interesting suggestion if you're bald. By using spirit gum from a costume shop, you can glue wig pieces on your head to resemble a Mohawk or something wild. Being bald has been pretty creative and fun for me since I do DRAG stunts like this with my character."*

Jaeda Fuentes, *"I usually mix it up. I like ponytails and use my hair and wigs for that, but I also like to use lace fronts when I'm a bit more lazy."*

"Where should you purchase your wig?"

BJ Stephens, *"I have a Wig America account, and eBay can sometimes have something. Don't just shop. "DRAG Queen" and look for a deal."*

Tiffani Middlesexx, *"Anywhere but a flea market."*

Felicia Fox, *"Beauty supply stores."*

Amy DeMilo, *"houseofbeauty.com and wigamerica.com"*

Lady Clover Honey, *"In New York, the stores are so expensive, so I buy online and have even found good places on eBay. You can find excellent quality at good prices.*
"

"Have you ever caught something from a used wig?"

Horchata, *"Never. I have yet to have that happen, knock on wood. But, if I buy a used wig, it's gonna get sanitized until the moon rises in the right position and the candle light flame burns toward it."*

Jade Shanell, *"It's like buying used underwear from an old person. Never buy used wigs. You never know what surprises you may find that you don't want"*

Selina Kyle, *"I've never caught anything from a wig. I've borrowed and lent my wigs to many people, but I usually explain to them that I don't want what they have, and if they don't want what I have, then they might not want to borrow it. Of course I don't have anything, but it's still nice to make sure they are not going to come back at you."*

Cherry Darling, *"I feel ill"*

 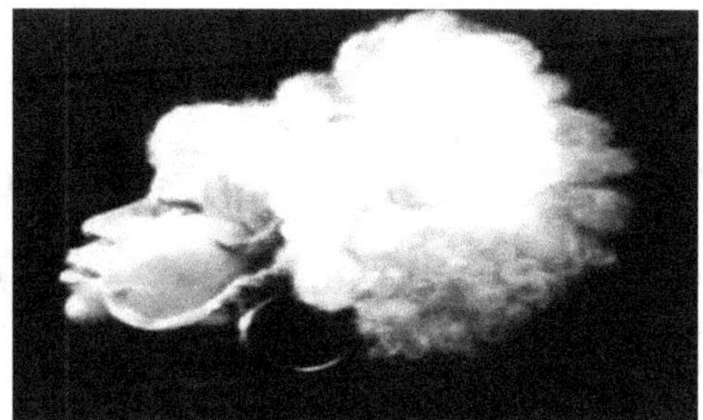

"How much do you pay for wigs?"

The performers stated they paid from $10 to $1,500 for a wig. On average, $47 is the price paid.

"Can you name three things most people do wrong when acquiring wigs?"

Amanda Love, *"They don't have the wig stretched prior to wearing it. People don't realize wigs are made for women, whose heads are smaller than men's. Also, not knowing how to style the hair correctly. Too much hairspray can kill your wig quickly. I learned this the hard way."*

Misty Eyez, *"Buying cheap costume wigs from Party City, etc. Applying oil sheen, unless it's human hair. Wearing it fresh out of the box, unsettled."*

Dmentia Divinyl, *"Brushing or combing a wig without any lubrication such as moisturizer or conditioner to keep them from getting too frayed looking. Cutting them when they have no business using a pair of scissors since they are not a beautician or hair stylist, or because they saw a Gaga video and* *got creative. Washing a wig with soap and water and expecting it to look like it came right off Zsa Zsa Gabor's head."*

Glitz Glam, *"They don't blend their own hair or pay attention to the back of their head. Set it too far back and leaves an awkward hair line."*

"How did you determine which color wig fit your style the best, as in if you had to choose one color for a wig, what would it be and why?"

J. P. Patrick, *"In 1988, I discovered a very high end wig company who produced a blond wig with dark roots. That is my signature color."*

Cathy Craig, *"Girl, try them all. A different color for a different mood."*

Conundrum, *"I have always picked something out of the ordinary like pink or something with highlights to stand out. But I also really like black because of my fair skin. It kind of brings that snow white look to me."*

Jae Chant, *"I would say look at your skin tone. I don't believe that one specific color suits only certain people. DRAG is about fun, wear what you want. And, if your thing is to glue a pony tail on your bald head, so be it...my best friend does this."*

Lady Clover Honey, *"Cause I'm a blonde, I do blond jokes and channel Marilyn, Mae West, Carol Channing and a young Goldie Hawn. What choice do I have? I like a golden, honey, champagne tone, but sometimes go with something lighter."*

"What wig of yours has the most history?"

Champagne T. Bordeaux, *"I just retired my twelve year old Whitney wig...poor thang!"*

Tiffani Middlesexx, *"I would have to say my Patti LaBelle do. It's older than dirt, but still looks and performs fabulously. Oh, wait a minute; am I talking about the wig or me?"*

Lady Tajma Hall, *"I have a bag full of wigs with history. I call them my lucky pageant wigs. I use them as bumps under my pageant hair. I have had them since I won my first national title in 1997."*

Beverly LaSalle, *"The one wig of mine that has the most history is the first one I ever purchased. I still have it to this day. It was a $20 wig from a costume shop. At this point, it is close to 20 years old."*

Patrice Knight, *"I would say my Tina Turner wig which I got when I was 24 and I used for almost 10 years before its ugly demise in a clothes dryer."*

"What is the wildest wig you own and what makes it wild?"

Maxine Padlock, *"That would be my huge blond wig made with four wigs. People used to ask how many puppies were killed to make it"*

Mis Sadistic, *"The wildest wig I own is my Amy Winehouse wig. It is 3 feet tall. I styled it myself out of one of my old Cher wigs. It is over the top even next to Miss Winehouse. I have a blast every time I wear it and so does the crowd."*

Jade Daniels, *" I'm not one to wear crazy looking hair, so my wildest one would be the one that is Ginormous. It is a big curly wig that is the equivalent of about 5 wigs put together and has about 7 different colors in it."*

Bukkake Blaque London St James, *"My favorite and wildest wig I have is my big white super hero wig. It takes 8 hours to curl it. You can get about 3 wears out of it before you have to set it again. It's the cheapest wig I own and the best. I make ribbon curls on it and it is fab."*

"How do you store your wigs?"

Brooklyn Bisette, *"On a wig stand...away from other queens."*

Jocelyn Summers, *"In a ball in the bottom of my DRAG bag. I have too much to carry each time I do a show to be putting it on a wig head and carrying it all over the place."*

Jami Michaels, *"On wig heads, some at the club, some here at home."*

Lacey Lynn Taylors, *"I built custom pegboards. A long wide piece of wood with large pegs spaced 10 inches apart. The wigs go on Styrofoam heads, the head onto a peg, and the pegboard onto several shelves in my closet. Styled hair can be so easily damaged, so proper storage on a wig head is a must."*

Babette Schwartz, *"My hair-dos are huge, so they stay on heads. I try to store them as high as possible to keep small animals from nesting in them."*

Raquel Payne, *"I try to keep most of my up dos and bigger rooted wigs on heads on a shelf. The long curly ones get hung on hooks to prevent frizz and curl manipulation. The short ones and straight ones get turned inside out and thrown in a bin. They can always be sprayed with oil sheen and brushed out fine."*

"How many wigs do you own?"
Based on responses, the average number is thirty-six wigs.

"How do you clean your wigs?"

Brooklyn Bisette, *"In the washing machine... just kidding. By hand in the sink with laundry detergent and then hang to dry in the shower."*

Alex Serpa, *"Soak it in Murphy's Oil to get the hair spray out. I use dishwashing detergent to remove the makeup. Makeup is grease paint and dishwashing detergent removes grease. I wash it by hand with laundry detergent and after rinsing, I let it soak in fabric softener for a day or two. After drying, I spray a little lemon Pledge on it to give the shine back. Most queens tend to wash synthetic wigs as if it was real hair using shampoo and conditioner. Synthetic hair is plastic so it needs to be treated accordingly."*

Horchata, *"I treat it like it's my own hair, sometimes. But, most times like a whore washing her panties in the sink with shampoo."*

Kori Stevens, *"Everyone says be gentle, but I have been doing this for 15 years and I am going to tell you my secret. Ammonia. Soak the wig in ammonia and all the products will come out, hairspray, spray color, spirit and bonding glue, it will all come out. Dunk the wig a few times, then rinse it out. After that, soak it in water and fabric softener, dunk it a few times, then rinse it out and hang it upside down to dry."*

Esme Russell, *"Shampoo and conditioner or I use Woolite. I hang them upside down to dry, and then restyle."*

"What do you do with the wig when you retire it?"

J. P. Patrick, *"They die horrible deaths. Straight into the trash. Although, they are long dead before they make it there."*

Alexis de la Mer, *"I usually donate them to my DRAG daughters to help them out."*

Selina Kyle, *"I usually store them, but sometimes I give them to DRAG queens just starting out, with friendly advice. I usually make sure that it's a queen who is interested in performing, but can't really afford it. I'm a softie when it comes to helping those who can't really help themselves. I've been in that position and I have always been thankful to queens who earnestly helped me with no ulterior motive."*

Patricia Grand, *"I have passed many on to young performers."*

Ashleigh Cooley, *"Give them away to friends that need them more than I."*

Whistle-stop Original, Official DRAG Handbook tour has
Jesus Poom joining John Behr in Southwest Florida

Chapter Nine Photos: First Image: Tian IconicShot, Second Image: Loc Robertson.

Chapter Ten

Eyewear

There are three types of eyewear for a performer

- The performer that has to wear glasses or contacts to function,
- The performer that selects glasses based on the character that they wish to portray,
- The performer that selects an eye color based on their attire or appearance.

Lady Tajma Hall, *"I wear designer shades for certain numbers to create the look I am going for. I think any types of glasses are a personal choice and should be used at your discretion."*

Dmentia Divinyl, *"I only used old lady glasses that are festive and funny and retro from time to time. My advice is to take out the lenses in case they fall or you fall with them and they break. If you wear real glasses, wear contacts instead for your performance. If you must wear glasses, then wear that elastic strap that attaches to them so they don't fall off. As nerdy as you may look, you'll thank me later."*

Pussy LaHoot, *"I have worn glasses since I was in the 5th grade. I only wear them in DRAG when I am driving. I am blind as a bat on stage. There was one time I wore contacts on stage and freaked out watching the people watching me. I like them when they are just blurry outlines holding out money."*

Anastasia Fallon, *"I get contacts from Paramount Wigs here in Tampa, Florida. The woman who normally works there loves the queens that come in, and she's always extra helpful. She has a range of prices for lenses, depending on your taste, up to about $60 for more dramatic looks."*

Jade Shanell, *"I get contacts from body jewelry online. I do not always wear them. When I do, I wear the aqua blue that glow in the dark. They give that Queen of the night look."*

Raquel Payne, *"I sometimes use colored contacts. I buy mine from hauntedeyes.com. They are great, never have any problems with them. The contacts add a stunning touch to a painted face. They also aid in becoming another person. You change the look of everything else, why not the eye color as well?"*

Name this performer without checking on

DRAG411.com

Chapter Ten Photos:colorcontactlens.com

Chapter Eleven

Pageants

Female impersonators select performing for various reasons. A few of them are very serious. Many of the entertainers have fun performing in front of an audience. Somewhere in between, everyone else falls. Along the way, for one reason or the other, the performers that often started their craft in local talent shows will pick up their game to search for a pageant. DRAG411 also created the book, Volume 3: "Crown Me!" by DRAG411.com "Winning Pageants."

This list is updated from the chapter created by Freddy Prinze.

Pageants fall into four categories. The local bar that has an open invitation to all that enter. A prelim for a particular town that leads up to a national title. A regional competition such as a state or territory leading up to a national title. A national title, that can only be entered because the contestants successfully competed in the previous pageants.

Originally, I had printed out 420 responses asking performers to signify the contests and competitions in their neighborhood along with the titles to the pageants in which they had successfully completed. When it came time to type out this chapter, it dawned on me that not enough of the pageants had signed onto this initial handbook to verify the massive number of performer's claims.

At least a quarter of the photos being sent in to me included performers wearing crowns. Needless to say, within seconds, all four hundred-twenty comments became suspect, and I didn't have the resources to verify them.

Fortunately most of the major pageant owners responded promptly providing details of their systems nationwide. I found a great resource on CarrieFairfield.com. This list is updated from the chapter created by Freddy Prinze.

Continental

thebatonshowlounge.com/continental.html

- North Carolina
- Florida
- Georgia
- California
- Puerto Rico
- Illinois
- Ohio

- Indiana
- Iowa
- Kentucky
- New York
- Texas
- Michigan
- Minnesota
- Pennsylvania
- Tennessee
- Arizona
- West Virginia

Miss Continental
Miss Continental Elite
Miss Continental Plus
Mr Continental (bio boys)
Miss Black Continental Newcomer
Mr Black Continental
Miss Black Continental At Large
Miss Black Continental Klassik
Mr Black Continental At Large
Miss Ebony International
Miss Ebony International Newcomer
Mr Ebony International
Miss Ebony International Plus

EOY
eoy.net

- Ohio
- North Carolina
- Arizona
- Alabama

King EOY
Mr EOY

Miss Gay America

missgayamerica.com

- Tennessee
- Washington DC
- Missouri
- Maryland
- Arizona
- Louisiana
- Florida
- California
- Ohio
- Oklahoma
- Pennsylvania
- Texas
- Kansas
- Nor Carolina
- Arkansas
- Virginia
- Illinois

USofA

usofa.org

Miss Gay USofA
- Texas
- Iowa
- Wisconsin
- South Carolina
- Puerto Rico
- Pennsylvania
- New York
- Oklahoma
- Arizona
- North Carolina
- Georgia
- Iowa
- Ohio
- Missouri
- Arkansas
- Massachusetts
- Tennessee
- Florida

Miss Gay USofA Classic
- Wisconsin
- Pennsylvania
- Arkansas
- Arizona
- Kansas
- Oklahoma
- Texas
- Ohio
- Louisiana
- Missouri
- New York

Miss Gay USofA At Large
- Florida
- Georgia
- Wisconsin
- Illinois
- Louisiana
- Maryland
- Missouri
- Arizona
- Iowa
- Oklahoma
- Texas
- Ohio
- North Carolina
- Kentucky

Miss Gay USofA Newcomer
- Arizona
- California
- Texas
- Florida
- Illionois
- Missouri
- New Mexico
- Ohio
- Oklahoma
- Tennessee
- Wisconsin

Mr Gay USofA

- Arizona
- Florida
- Iowa
- Texas
- New Mexico
- North Carolina
- Oklahoma
- Wisconsin

Mr Gay USofA At Large

- Florida
- Oklahoma
- Texas
- Wisconsin

Mister USofA MI misterusofami.com

- California
- Tennessee
- Arizona
- Florida
- Arkansas
- Oklahoma
- Ohio
- Colorado
- Indiana
- Louisiana
- Missouri
- Georgia

Mister USofA MI Classic

- Texas
- Florida
- Arkansas

Miss Diva USofA

- Texas
- Oklahoma

All American Goddess

allamericangoddess.com

- Florida
- Ohio
- Texas
- Tennessee
- Louisiana
- New Mexico
- Pennsylvania
- Indiana
- North Carolina
- South Carolina
- Missouri
- Michigan

All American Goddess At Large

- Florida
- Ohio
- Texas
- Louisiana
- Alabama
- Tennessee
- Indiana
- North Carolina
- Missouri

Master Male Illusionist

– no prelims   mastermaleillusionist.com

American National Star

facebook.com/AmericanNationalStarPageantry

- Arizona
- Missouri
- Oklahoma
- Arizona

Miss American National Star
Mr American National Star
Mr Butch American National Star
Miss Vintage American National Star
Miss Femme American National Star

More information (and conversations with actual National Pageant winners can be found in Volume 3, "Crown Me!"

Hundreds of invitations sent to the titleholders, pageant promoters, judges, and talent show hosts to share their insight on not only winning pageants and contests but also owning the stage every time they perform. Their topics included auxiliary steps to success needed for song selection, dancing, movement on stage, props, backup dancers, creating your own edge, personal interviews, steps to success for winning the talent category every time you step on stage, on stage questions, evening wear, and creative costuming. They discussed in their own unedited words, wardrobe changes, makeup, hair, shoes, when is the time to compete, qualities needed for a judge, and the top misconceptions of contestants competing in the pageantry systems.

Commentary shared with Todd Kachinski Kottmeier included national leaders: AJ Menendez, Amy Demilo, Anastacia Dupree, Anson Reign, Bob Taylor, Breonna Tenae, Brittany T Moore, Coco Montrese, Dana Douglas, Darryl Kent, Denise Russell, Dey Jzah Opulent, Freddy Prinze Charming, Gage Gatlyn, Jay Santana , Jayden Knight, Jennifer Foxx, Joey Jay,

Kori Stevens, Mis Sadistic, Mykul Jay Valentine, Natasha Richards, Rico Taylor, Sam Hare, Stephanie Stuart, Taina T. Norell, Tiffani Middlesexx, Tori Taylor, Ty Nolan, Vinnie Marconi, and Vivika D'Angelo. From DRAG411, the largest organization for male and female impersonators, with over 6,000 entertainers in 32 countries.

Mis Sadistic, *"It is a very costly venture to participate in pageants. Entry fees range from $25 to $500 and up. Hotels are from $79 per night to $200 and up. Food $50 per day at least, not including drinks. Travel $100 per day, taxi or car rental, trip or travel insurance $75 and up. Major travel airfare or sea voyage $150 to $1,000. Costuming $250 and up, dresses $500 and up. Props, backdrops, sets $1,000 and up. Back up dancers $50 each and up. Animal rentals $1,000 and up. Please keep in mind these are rough numbers. It all depends on title you are competing. Some of the crowns and the prize that goes along with them are very large. The entry and everything that goes with it is relative."*

CoCo Montrese, *"It costs approximately $2,000 to $5,000 to enter a national pageant when planning to go to win."*

Ginger Minj, *"When all is said and done, Miss Continental Plus will cost roughly $8,000 this year. Last year totaled $4,000 and the year before was about $2,000. The more you want to win, the more you put into it. The closer you are, the more it takes. Local pageants are generally much less cost-prohibitive."*

Nova Starr, *"Pageants can have some serious costs. Any wise contestant should consider these costs before entering any pageant, especially if it is a preliminary to a national pageant. If you qualify, you are REQUIRED to attend the national pageant, and sometimes prize money and promoters alone cannot carry you through."*

Maxine Padlock, *"I was in a pageant and had asked the bars I have worked at and the people and other businesses in the area. I even had people at work throw a little fundraiser for me, at which I did a number for them and they helped with my shoes and accessories."*

Daphne Ferraro, *"I had supporters like Timothy Hickman of Orlando. He used to own Florida America and was a dedicated friend and supporter of the America system. Also, Brent Silvers of Tampa. He was my partner for 6 years and promoter for about 4 of those as well. He continues to love DRAG and supports many contestants, and we remain great friends."*

Amy DeMilo, *"When I compete I hold fundraisers and benefits in the clubs I work for. Honey Pot, Hamburger Mary's, Chelsea and Georgie's Alibi have all sponsored me. Also, the best support is your personal promoter if you're lucky enough to have one."*

Patricia Mason, *"I like to depend on myself as much as possible. I have been criticized for NOT asking for help, but what is wrong with trying to accomplish things on your own? I have had a few sponsors who have stepped up and said they want to help me. I am always honored and flattered that they want to assist. I have a few close friends who I know I can count on for things, but most of the time, I will get things myself."*

Name the performers without checking on DRAG411.com

Chapter Twelve

Music

We asked performers to list
25 sources for music for their acts.

- YouTube
- A helpful DJ
- iTunes
- FYE
- Hear it on the radio
- Amazon.com
- Overstock.com collections
- Bar collections
- Movies
- TV Shows
- Reality Shows
- Playlist.com
- Frostwire.com
- Pandora
- My Space
- Yahoo Music
- Limewire
- Billboard
- Customer request
- Friend suggestions
- Napster
- Barnes & Noble
- Rhapsody
- Stealing other acts (oops, I mean they inspired me)

Photo: Image: Idea go / FreeDigitalPhotos.net

Chapter Thirteen

Clothes are for Closets

**My clothes can also be found on my Sofa,
my chairs, my dining room table,
back of my toilet, trunk of my car...”**

Beyond the internet, name a few places in your neighborhood to locate costumes

- Thrift stores, USA
- House of Make Believe, Clearwater, Florida
- On Point Dance Studio, St Petersburg, Florida
- Ross & Ross Outlets, USA
- Avenue, USA
- Payless Shoes, USA
- GBS, Fort Lauderdale, Florida
- Phoenix Boom Boom, Phoenix, Arizona
- Skyscraper Heels, Chicago, Illinois
- Head and Threads, Chicago, Illinois
- Beatnix, Chicago, Illinois
- Torrid, Brandon, Florida
- Rainbow, Tucson, Arizona
- Marshalls, USA
- Ritzy Rags, Orlando, Florida
- Century Costumes, Orlando, Florida
- A T Jones, Baltimore,Maryland
- The Wig Center, Baltimore,Maryland
- Renas Wild Wear, Tampa, Florida
- Features Costumes, Tampa, Florida
- MC Films, Tampa, Florida
- Nicole's Beauty, Memphis, Tennessee
- Goodwill, USA
- Sunnys, Winter Haven, Florida
- Soul Train, Lakeland, Florida
- Beatniks, Miami, Florida
- Thomas Fashion and Bridal Sevierville, Tennessee
- Glamor Boutique, Las Vegas, Nevada
- Star Costume, Las Vegas, Nevada

- Williams Costume, Las Vegas, Nevada
- Consignment shops, USA
- The Costume Shop, Boise, Idaho
- Catwalk, Myrtle Beach, South Carolina
- Studio Lights, Denver, Colorado
- Raves, Denver, Colorado
- ImiJimi, Denver, Colorado
- Mischievous, Salt Lake City, Utah
- Decades, Salt Lake City, Utah
- Giggles, Sarasota, Florida
- Ragstock, Chicago, Illinois
- Bella Brazil Fashion Wear, Lakeland, Florida

Not everyone has a chance to shop retail. The internet has made it simple to shop while sitting in your Fruit of the Looms eating bonbons.

- Electriqueboutique.com
- eBay
- Craig's List
- queenoftheball.com
- amazon.com
- fredericks.com
- greatglam.com
- sequinqueen.com
- sexyshoes.com
- bordello.com
- wickedtemptations.com
- Summer Day
- Victoria's Secret
- highestheel.com
- discountdancesupply.com
- trannygear.com
- asos.com
- Samantha Mo
- Queen Diva Designs

The amount of money spent the first year depends greatly on the performer's budget. A performer that decides to take the high road of sequined gowns and authentic hair, will most likely not spend the same amount as a person borrowing items from his mother's closet. It is finding that compromise between what they desire, and the reality of their wallet, that will determine expenditures.

Deva DaVyne, *"I've spent so much more after my first year. I borrowed a lot of my dresses back then and only bought makeup. But now, I buy my own dresses or have them made. I wish I could learn how to sew."*

Horchata, *"Everything that I got was hand me downs or I just made them. Good thing that I can sew, but the material cost money. I would say I spent about $100 per month on stuff and accessories."*

Melissa Morgan, *"My mom and I made a lot of it, but still spent a lot on DRAG."*

Felina Cashmere, *"Not much. I went to the thrift stores and pieced clothing together and I stole my makeup from convenience stores, we all did. Plus, I raided my mother's closet."*

Diedra Windsor Walker, *"Who knows, who counts? I mean we don't all start out in Lucinda Holliday and designer gowns. It's about looking good and spending what it takes that you can afford."*

Mis Sadistic, *"I can't tell you a dollar amount, I sewed and glued and rhinestoned every show a new outfit. I made everything myself. The only thing it cost what seemed to be a lot back then, were the shoes. With that I learned a trick, spray paint. I was able to stretch out the shoes that way. Who has money in the beginning?"*

Joselyn Summers, *"More than I was making. This is not a cheap field to work in, and when you are 18 working in retail, a $50 wig seems like a huge purchase, not to mention clothes, shoes and accessories."*

Brianna Lee, *"OMG! Those credit cards were maxed out. I have no idea. Plastic at 16, hmmmm, you do the math."*

Amy DeMilo, *"Not much, everything was given to me or borrowed at first."*

Beverly LaSalle, *"Wow, that first year I must have spent thousands. Once I realized that this was not a choice to be taken lightly, I went and purchased everything so I could stand out, I wanted to have my own unique look. I also received some beautiful costumes as gifts from some of my dearest friends."*

Alisa Summers, *"The first year was the hardest. Building up a DRAG wardrobe from scratch is not easy. During my first year, I had my makeup case, with over $500 worth of cosmetics stolen. I'd say I spent well over a few thousand dollars just because of having to start from scratch."*

Babette Schwartz, *"Probably about $10.00. I was in college and broke. Everything came from thrift stores and friends closets. Luckily it was the 80's, and that vintage look was in."*

Summer Breeze, *"I can't put that in print, my husband would kill me."*

Over time you have no choice but to eliminate wardrobe based on wear and tear, shrinkage, theft and random excuses. Many performers often hold particular pieces past their prime based on sentimental reasons.

Melissa Morgan, *"My first pair of earrings that my real mom gave me when I started DRAG. She supports me very much."*

Anastasia Fallon, *"Absolutely, my favorite is my very first pair of jeans for the stage. I was all ready to do the newly released Pink single "Don't Let Me Get Me." So, I went to TJ Maxx and found the sickest pair of painted up punk style jeans, and those size nine's fit like magic. I looked flawless in them. I was 18. Haven't been that size since then, but I just can't get rid of the things."*

Rhyana Vorhman, *"I still have my first wig that my DRAG boss gave me. It's a reminder of where I started and who helped me. I will keep it always."*
Mis Sadistic, *"I did. I had a very dear friend, JoJo, that had given me a microphone made out of an electric toothbrush. He gave it to me as a prop,*

something to hold onto and to take my mind off the stage fright. It worked, I still take it to every show with me."

Patricia Mason, *"I have a one piece body suit that I still use. I remember going to Wal-Mart and buying it for the first time. It is full of holes, but I love it."*

Barbra Herr, *"Oh heavens no... It would have to be in the Smithsonian."*

Alisa Summers, *"The very first shoes I performed in were Baby Phat Converse-style sneakers covered in rhinestones. My DRAG mother read me about not wearing heels, so I never wore them for a show again. I still have them, in the box, good as new."*

Jay Santana, *"My first wig."*

Name this performer without checking on DRAG411.com

Juwana Jackson, *"I think I still have the first outfit I ever sewed."*

Esme Russell, *"My first costume was made for me by a queen in Miami named Lola Lush. It was a yellow tablecloth bought at Goodwill and she turned it into a costume. I still have it."*

Eunyce Raye, *"A Boa."*

Joey Brooks, *"I still have one of Brenda Dee's funnel caps of chiffon."*

ummer Breeze, *"I have two. One is a ruffled sequin jacket given to me by Kim Ross. The other is my first Liza outfit given to me by Bobbie Lake"*

Afeelya Bunz, *"My Granny Fat Suit"*

Pussy LaHoot, *"Earrings I had gotten after my grandmother died in 1971. I was only 10 but I loved the ruby glass clip on buttons, and I always asked her to wear them to church. She told me you only wear earrings at night, because they would shimmer in the moonlight."*

Blair Michaels, *"A gown made over 20 years ago for the coronation for Miss San Diego."*

Lady Sabrina, *"My very first dress. I remember because in those days big sizes weren't common, so I found this white dress on clearance. That damn dress is ugly to anyone else, but to me it was the beginning of something big. I owe that dress a lot."*

"Just because you use the ladies room Doesn't make you a lady."

The Infamous Todd Kachinski Kottmeier

Name the performers without checking on DRAG411.com

Chapter Thirteen Photos:
First Image: jscreationzs / FreeDigitalPhotos.net.

Name the performers without checking on
DRAG411.com

Chapter Fourteen

Next Chapter

The next chapter of this book is yet to be written. It sits in the reader's mind, his heart, and in HIS conversations, we will share. Creating this book just opened the door to free dialogue. It is hard to calculate or determine the path of this profession.

Misty Eyez, *"With the help of RuPaul and her DRAG Race, DRAG is on the forefront again and I think it will only rise. I think DRAG has a bright future."*

Champagne T. Bordeaux, *"Going stronger than ever. The youth are great, they are doing it, making themselves known and staying true to the craft."*

Amanda Love, *"I see it growing bigger and better and I see more of a nationwide following than what we already have."*

Amy DeMilo, *"There is no denying female impersonation is an art form. I hope in ten years everyone is able to realize it, appreciate it and respect it. Let's work on a retirement plan."*

Jay Santana, *"I hope that some of the competitiveness is gone and that it can be FUN again for those doing it."*

Glitz Glam, *"It's only just the beginning. I feel it's an underappreciated art form. With gay rights moving forward, recognition will follow, probably in the form of more main stream DRAG celebrities."*

Anita Cox, *"I believe it will go on stronger than ever."*

Barbra Seville, *"I think it will be more accepted by mainstream and less appreciated by the gay community."*

Name the performers without checking on
DRAG411.com

Chapter Fifteen

Performing

Designing a game plan to approach bars for your first gig is daunting. There are hundreds of ideas, but only a few actually work.

This chapter should not be confused with the chapter on bars. The bar chapter defines expectations of the venue to the performer. This chapter defines the performer to the audience. You would automatically assume that the goal of a performer and a bar owner would be the same, which is to spoil the bar's patrons. In this section the performer will learn that often those two goals are taken by far different paths.

Ginger Minj, *"My very first booking was a beautiful tragedy when I was just 16 years old. I used my cousin's boyfriend's ID, grabbed some of my sister's clothes, stopped at Walgreen's for some luxurious Cover Girl (which doesn't cover boy), and performed to the only CD I could find in my brother's car, the Batman soundtrack. I wouldn't attempt DRAG again for quite a few years."*

Jami Michaels, *"I was 16 years old at Power Company in Durham, North Carolina. The door person thought I was so cute, he let me in as 21. I walked in and saw this beautiful creature doing a number and I was captured from that very moment."*

BJ Stephens, *"I went to the Melody Club in Gainesville on a dare when I was 20 while a musical theater major in college. The girls really kept me on my toes. Thrown in the deep end, you gotta swim, or sink!"*

Mis Sadistic, *"The Ice Palace on Sundays had a talent show. I was out on Fire Island every weekend, I lived for it. I was always watching the girls in the dressing room, either helping or watching. Shirleena used to do a number where the DJ would speed up the track until she sounded like Minnie Mouse. It was so fast, and then he would slow it back down to normal for the finish. She never missed a word."*

Jade Daniels, *"I definitely remember them being special. I was lucky to have the support of my really close friends, and be in the company of some great entertainers that helped me to be the person and entertainer I am today. Now, when I see pictures from back then...that's a different thought."*

Wendy G. Kennedy, *" I started at Starlight by the Park in New Orleans at age 40, but 18 in my mind."*

Misty Eyez, *"I would go in and ask how I could help, or if they could use me"*

Anastasia Fallon, *"I entered talent nights like crazy my first year. Luckily, after my first performance, a friend saw me and recommended me to the bar that became my home for my first year. I had a steady gig until they closed."*

Maxine Padlock, *"I would show up in DRAG and then they usually ask if I have a number and ask me to perform and then go from there."*

Mis Sadistic, *"I won a contest and part of the prize was a booking at the venue The Silver Lining Cherry Lane in Queens, New York."*

Penelope Reigns, *"I was tagging along with other performers to smaller bars to get to know the owners."*

Jami Michaels, *"I actually got my first booking through a duet I did with my friend who was a friend who was a female impersonator at the time."*

Esme Russell, *"My first booking was through another queen who was better connected. Since then, I have networked myself."*

Stormy Vain, *"Hung at venues, supported the bar, bartenders & DJ's."*

Teri Courtney, *"I literally had to kick doors in."*

LaKeisha Pryce, *"I was a regular so I got to know the show director, did a few talent shows, and earned my spot."*

Ina and Ineeda Twat, *"We usually mix and mingle with the bar/club crowd to get a feel of the venue before meeting the manager or owner."*

Barbra Seville, *"We made an audition video. This was a long time ago. They stared at us in disbelief and gave us a gig."*

Rickie Lee, *"I entered a talent show and won, worked that weekend, the rest is history. To get gigs, just pick up the phone and get your butt in there. Be persuasive and build yourself up. Don't be timid."*

Jaeda Fuentes, *"Mainly I get new gigs through word of mouth through other queens or being in the venue in DRAG and representing myself in a positive way. People are always watching and owners and managers see that."*

Babette Schwartz, *"I usually ply the management with baked goods and lots of sweet talk."* (Author's note: Funny, I hired people that used this cookie treat on me too)

Determining the distance that you will drive is often based on your desire to perform. Most performers stated that they seldom drove more than two hours. Only 3% of the performers had the bragging rights to have job offers from Paris, London, Rio de Janeiro, Hawaii, Alaska and Boise, Idaho.

Lady Liemont and Mis Sadistic on the tour stop

Not every venue is a gay bar. Ninety-seven percent of the performances take place in a gay bar, so for this chapter we are primarily focusing in on their venues. Let me note at this time, to get it out of the way, that 3.48% of the survey's participants were straight. This leads me to believe that the stereotype of many men wearing dresses, leads more credence to cross-dressing than performing. A performer entering a bar is selling their style. It is their uniqueness that intrigues the bar manager into hiring them.

Jessica Jade, *"I am known for having big crazy hair."*

BJ Stephens, *"I love to do comedy numbers, but I really love singing live."*

Deva DaVyne, *"I'm known for my splits and back flips. I'm also known for grabbing a guy out of the audience and playing with him."*

Amanda Love, *"I'm known for doing a lot of country, but I am known for my ability to adapt and apply comedy into any number. I involve the audience with my performance. Sometimes it takes balls to be a woman and dressed as a simple housewife wearing an apron. The apron had a towel sewn into the front of it, and when you lift the towel out pops a huge penis and a huge set of balls. The crowd loved it and I would have audience members on stage with me to perform the song. We had a blast."*

PurrZsa Kyttyn, *"The cat sound I do. I actually had the humane society called on me because someone thought I was torturing a cat, and I had to make the noise for the police and animal control."*

Stormy Vain, *"I'm known for my big colorful wigs."*

Monique Michaels, *"I am known for a level of vintage style and class, even when performing something bawdy or dirty or sexy."*

Ima and Ineeda Twat, *"Our matching clothes, big hair and makeup. Sometimes our shows can get a little risqué."*

The average performer does fifteen shows a month including non-profits. It gives them many opportunities to refine their persona. We asked them, **""You are getting ready to go on stage. The lights dim, the music queues up. An announcer crackles across the sound system that you are about to enter the stage..."**

"Ladies and gentlemen, please welcome the twenty-five dancing toes of Kori Stevens."

"Please give it up long and hard, just the way she likes it. Your friend, and my best friend, Miss Vivika D'Angelo."

"This old hooker, you know who she is...Amanda Love."

"Ladies and gentlemen, whether you like it or not...Pandora DeStrange."

"She couldn't make it on RuPaul's DRAG Race, so she is Rainbow Lounge's welfare child. Give it up for the horrible, big as a house, Mystique Summers."

"Ladies, Gentlemen, and Gentlemen that are Ladies, please welcome to the stage Miss Beverly LaSalle."

"Ladies and gents, watch your personal belongings here comes Cherry Darling."

"She is your diamond diva, your Haitian bombshell, the face that broke a thousand hearts. Welcome to the stage the sensational talents of Cartier Paris."

"Here she is, your cunty congeniality, your flexy red devil of Ohio...Scarlett Fever."

"Please welcome the man of many faces, Mr. Kenneth Blake."

"She's big, she's bold, she's brassy and sassy...Miss Eunyce Raye."

"Ladies and gentlemen, buckle up your seats and get ready for the ride of your life. The dancing toes of Miss Shae Shae LaReese."

"Here to set the stage on fire and to bewitch your minds. Ladies and gentlemen, welcome to her throne, the home wrecker of the south, Miss Raquel Payne."
"The Sex Goddess of Northwest Arkansas, Miss Jenna Chambers Tisdale."

"Ladies and gentlemen, please welcome to the stage the last of the red hot mommas, every truck driver's best friend, Miss Pussy LeHoot."

Carol Burnett had one, Bob Hope, and even Sonny and Cher. Often, a song says more about an entertainer than any words from an announcer. Occasionally, performers will select songs based on their persona.

Kori Stevens, *"Last Dance is what comes to mind. It's a song that no matter how tired I am or how much pain I am in, I am going to perform the hell out of it. It's the weirdest thing, and other people have said it as well, but when that song starts something comes over me and I am a young boy again."*

Mis Sadistic, *"I Will Survive by Gloria Gainer. It gets me through the good times and the bad ones too."*

Jade Shanell, *"Beyonce's Fever, because baby when I come in a room, you're going to feel like you have a fever, hot and bothered."*

Alexis De La Mer, *"Proud from Queer as Folk. It's a feel good song."*

Pandora DeStrange, *"Sweet Transvestite. After the first time I saw Rocky Horror Picture Show my life was changed forever."*

Beverly LaSalle, *"My theme song is Celine Dion's Colour Of My Love. It's an amazing song and really expresses my feelings to my audience that comes out to see me perform."*
Mr. Kenneth Blake, *"I'm Still Standing & What Makes a Man a Man."*

Danika Fierce, *"My theme song would be Not Myself Tonight. It's so true."*

Pussy LeHoot, *"The theme from the Golden Girls, Thank You For Being A Friend."*

Rickie Lee, *"I Know I'll Never Love This Way Again by Dionne Warwick."*

After a year of performing, the performers tend to work through most of their difficulties to come up with a routine. As they look back, they discover lessons learned.

"My goal
is to always come from a place of love
...but sometimes you just have to break it down
for a motherf*cker"
RuPaul

Lady Tajma Hall, *"If I had to do it all over again, I would say NO! It was not as easy as people made it out to be. I am happy now that I did it, but I am not sure I would have done it had I known the REAL story."*

Madisyn de la Mer, *"Trust no one. And, don't leave your bags unattended. Shit will go missing or get tampered with. I've seen girls crush light bulbs into another performer's Coty powder."*

CoCo Montrese, *"Experience is the best teacher."*

Conundrum, *"I would not change a thing. I believe I am who I am today because of what I have experienced. Now I know what works for me and what simply does not."*

Cherry Darling, *"I would have got rid of the eyebrows a lot earlier honey! All that sticky wax was like a smear of dry jizz."*

Dmentia Divinyl, *"I have learned that we are worth a lot more money as far as booking fees go, and to request a higher standard of hotel accommodations for safety and security as a DRAG diva traveling across the country like a circus freak."*

Rusti Fawcett, *"Keep my mouth closed and my ears open. There were a lot of people I "could" have learned from."*

Kitty D'Meaner, *"I believe I have progressed at my own pace and will continue to do so. I still struggle with finding the time to get my face out there and perform, but everything in time. I'm proud of myself, I wouldn't change a thing."*

Vegas Platinum, *"Let my attitude and cockiness take a back seat. It takes time to perfect the art of illusion. The one thing I wish I had learned a lot sooner is humility. It will get you a long way in this industry where many seasoned professionals and people who have been doing DRAG for 30 years are everywhere. Know you haven't proven yourself to most of them, respect their history and where they've been."*

Jaeda Fuentes, *"The only change I would make was not quitting DRAG for a man. I stopped doing DRAG for an ex-boyfriend for 4 months because he didn't like it. If he can't appreciate me, then he doesn't need to be in my life."*

*It is said, like teaching, performing has more to
do with passion than a paycheck. A performer starting
has no paycheck; hoping to get to the industry
$50 per show (plus tips).*

Madisyn de la Mer, *"I work usually
for tips only or the prize at talent contests.
You should earn your way to the top, and never act like
you're too good for anything. Exposure is everything.
Do every benefit show you can, and always show face
in public."*

Naomi Wynters, *"I'd say it depends on the venue. Some treat new girls
equally, and other venues treat you as a new girl and you may get a smaller
rate. I'm torn on this answer having mostly worked for a club, or had an inner
association to my booking. I wouldn't even know what a fair estimate would
be."*

Jocelyn Summers, *"I did free shows for a long time just to build my name
and craft. Even after that, DRAG is not going to pay the bills for years. When
we do start making money, it ends up getting invested right back into the
gig. The early years are about building a wardrobe and repertoire that will
help you build your career to its maximum potential."*

BJ Stephens, *"What you bring to the party impacts what you get. I think $50
and up is a good start. Tips make up a big part, but you gotta work."*
Ororo, *"I was doing it for free, then when I started to get a booking fee, it
was enough to cover transportation. I didn't start getting paid until I proved
myself as entertaining."*

Lady Tajma Hall, *"The amount a new performer can expect to make in the
first few years depends on the dedication and seriousness of the performer.
If you work really hard, promote yourself, listen, learn and apply yourself,
you can be very successful the first few years.*

Pandora DeStrange, *"In my
opinion, you should create art for art's sake. Once you have fine-tuned your
craft, the money will come. Most performers start performing because they
have to. It is in their blood, not just to get a pay check."*

Conundrum, *"Unless you are a professional with makeup, hair performance and designing from the get go, chances are you will not be making much money right away. Even If you are great at all these things, you still need to get your name out there before people start to book you."*

Danika Fierce, *"I'm in my first year, and all I can really say is, it's like serving. You make the amount of money that you want to make. It's all about costumes, music, attitude and performance."*

Kitty D'Meaner, *"It's a hard business to break into. In my experience, you need to shell out money to make money. You have to put the time and funds in to get yourself out there and noticed. Some can get bookings right off the bat. Others, like myself, have to work at it. You have to love the performance and what you do first. If the passion is there, the check will come, eventually."*

Babette Schwartz, *"A newbie should not expect to earn rent and car payment. This craft is very much about building a name and a following. I have two other jobs besides performing."*

"In a community of queens, pessimism is king. "
Steve Hammond

It is strange that in such a negative environment personal optimism flourishes. I can pull nine performers out of a dressing room, and ask them privately (91.87%), "describe the remaining people inside the room." Those nine people will terrorize the character of the people left inside the room. Those same people, when asked where they see themselves or the profession in a decade, will excitedly explain incredibly new heights.

Jade Shanell, *"I see myself still doing DRAG in ten years, and being even better at it. Hopefully one day I will be just as big as RuPaul or Lady Bunny."*

Misty Eyez, *"I would love to be a DRAG queen on The View, or Oprah."*

Lola Honey, *"I am the Tina Turner of DRAG. I'll be doing this until my legs fall off, and then I'll do it some more."*

Barbra Herr, *"Well, if I'm still performing in ten years, I see myself looking like Joan Rivers with every facelift known to man. Otherwise...retired."*

Melody Mayhem, *"I'm always up to date with music and fashion. I'm thankful for my genes, I look ages younger. So I'm sure I'll still be one of those fierce queens of the area. The big mistake other queens make is that they* *get stuck in their era, and younger crowds and audiences don't feel them so much. It's always about the next generation."*

Echo Dazzle, *"In ten years I will be an old wrinkled crone."*

Kitty D'Meaner, *"I've never looked at female impersonation as a career choice. I do it purely for the release and the fun of it. In ten years I may still need the release or I may not."*

BukkakeBlaque London St James, *"I hope to still be in the business in ten years. I hope to be in a different light than I am now. Now, I perform three days a week, about ten numbers a week and still have to have a full time job just to make ends meet. I am laying groundwork to have my own show and still be able to travel and meet all of the great people that are in our world. The craft and artistry of DRAG is a very personal thing, and I hope to find and explore that within myself to the fullest."*

Jaeda Fuentes, *"I actually have big goals with my career and I do have a ten year plan. In ten years I will be in a muu muu at a retirement home in Palm Springs."*

Every wave of performers that surge through a decade ultimately creates change. The day's pre LOGO TV, will not be the same ten years from now. The acceptance by mainstream society will have changed just as the culture has assimilated over the past two decades. Changes in the past twenty years are not evident by 62.12% of today's female impersonators. Most of them are oblivious to the struggles of performing twenty years ago, when it was still illegal in most counties for men to be wearing dresses in a bar.

Mis Sadistic, *"In almost twenty years I have watched female impersonation go from being one of the most respected parts of the gay community to a tolerated part of the gay community. There are many reasons this has happened and no one group of people can be blamed. I am hopeful that things are starting to turn around and the respect is being restored."*

BJ Stephens, *"I'm an OLLLDDD Gal. I've seen the evolution from "showgirl" to "real girl" and now it's going back. Everything is a pendulum."*

Mis Sadistic, *"When I started over thirty years ago, DRAG was over the top, bigger than life. That includes wigs, costumes, etc. DRAG evolved into hormones and silicone girls. If you didn't have breasts, it was hard to get work. Now we have become a beautiful mix of everything and room for all. We have come a long way. I remember a time when you wouldn't think of saying I want to be a DRAG queen for a profession. People considered us as having a mental disorder."*

Melissa Morgan, *"Wow! OK I'm 38. And that's cool. I have seen styles change and music and so many things."*

Amy DeMilo, *"We are seen in the public eye more than ev thanks to television talk shows, sitcoms and movies. Also, you to places like Hamburger Mary's, Lucky Changs and RuPaul's DRAG Race. Like everything and everyone, we are still evolving."*

Barbra Herr, *"The glam is gone. Seems like anyone gets up on stage and performs not knowing their material, not respecting the glamour that DRAG is supposed to be. These performers will not have longevity in this business. I've been around for 38 years...I've seen the best."*

Jami Michaels, *"I celebrated 20 years this year. I look back; I see that as a society we have come so far that there is no longer the need to go to gay bars as there was in the 90's. The art of female impersonation used to be something taboo and people would come out just for that reason. These days, nothing is taboo."*

Danilo De La Torre, *"DRAG is now mainstream. That wasn't the case twenty years ago."*

Rusti Fawcett, *"Attitude and arrogance from some of the children who don't realize if not for us, they might not have the privileges they have now."*

Joey Brooks, *"DRAG was more over the top back then, big costumes, big hair. These days, the performers just want to look like a girl."*
Teri Courtney, *"Twenty years ago there was a lot more respect for the entertainers. Rightly so, we earned it. Today many young entertainers feel "entitlement" in show business. It has always been about paying your dues, and our youth is clueless to this."*

Rickie Lee, *"OMG, so many. Makeup is better, songs have changed, and freedom to be is more widespread. Laws have changed. When I first started, if you were caught on the street in DRAG, there was a fine, and you were lucky if you were not carted off to jail. Things have vastly improved."*

Often, performing is just the luck of being at the right place at the right time. Perhaps a bar has a full cast. Everything changes as a slot opens. The entertainer is offered a number due to a cancellation of a performer. Time to time, being in the right place at the right time, offers you the possibility to perform in an audience far above the capacity of the bar where you entertain. Gay Pride events from parades to the staged events have opened the art to massive gay audiences. No matter how pretty they are, no matter how talented, well- rehearsed, or experienced, eventually something will go wrong. Even the most seasoned performers on earth cannot avoid when disaster strikes. We watch on TV as entertainers pass out from the heat, Presidents vomit, and singers forget words; female impersonators are not any different.

BJ Stephens, *"I was working in an outside stage environment, stepped off the stage, my heels sunk into the earth, and I pitched forward onto my face just as the song began."*

Deva DaVyne, *"I was hosting a DRAG show one night and in the middle of my opening number I went to do my signature back flip into a split when I felt my bra clasp snap. Next thing I knew, my inserts were flying into the crowd, and my bra hit the floor at the same time as I landed. I was mortified, but I kept on performing and still got tipped really well."*

Vivika D'Angelo, *"Hosting a benefit show and I was out talking on the microphone when I realized I had forgotten to tuck properly and my junk was showing. It was not cute."*

Amanda Love, *"I was doing my signature number "Redneck Woman." I was in the middle of the number and the skirt I was wearing was a tad too big so I had it safety pinned together at the waist to keep it up. I went into a spin and the pin came undone and there I stood in front of the bar with nothing on below the waist but my hose and duct tape."*

Ada Buffet, *"While performing in a local bar, I hopped up to "walk the bar" and my hair got caught in the ceiling fan. Took my wig right off and spin, spin, spin. I left it there and continued my number. It eventually flew off on its own."*

Naomi D'Lish, *"One night we blew a fuse and had no lights for the stage. After the host was vamping for a while, I figured I'd had enough and could do just fine with just a candle. I did a song called "God Loves Ugly" by Jordin Sparks and lit mostly my face with a bar candle as I danced on stage. People still talk about it today. It was just what I felt like I had to do to keep the crowd happy and still make tips while I was at it."*

Selina Kyle, *"I was still a young performer and trying to get on cast at a local club. I had used antiperspirant on my face to keep from sweating and had gotten a tiny bit in my eye. It continued to soak up all the moisture from my eye the whole night. I didn't let that stop me. I got on stage, giving the audience mostly a profile shot the whole night because that eye was redder than Satan's c**k. But, the show went on, and so did I."*

Melody Mayheim, *"I forgot to remove the gum from my mouth. As I was lip synching, it somehow flew out of my mouth and landed right in someone's hair."*

Shae Shae LaReese, *"My top came down during a pageant, during the talent competition. I never stopped, the audience stood up on their feet when I finished. I was topless, and won all three categories."*

Glitz Glam, *"Once, at Garage in Tampa, Florida, I was swinging from a swing above the bar and we were always supposed to have our feet up. I accidentally nailed a bartender in the head with my stiletto. OOPS!"*

Raquel Payne, *"Driving home one night in DRAG after a booking, my DRAG sister and I were hit by a drunk driver. Our vehicle went spinning across the* *intersection. Luckily, we weren't hurt and neither was the drunk driver. Though he thought we were women, we told him the truth to avoid any altercation. My DRAG bag went flying through the air, showering the streets with wigs, heels, and rolls of duct tape. All the EMT's and police were really sweet and helpful. The vehicle now rests in pieces, but we are alive and well. Not even that can keep a good girl down."*

Dee Gregory, *"I was performing a trio of tunes from "Starlight Express" and at one point I was walking backward alongside the catwalk expecting to stop just before the stage front. I had gotten off at an angle and walked into the side of the catwalk, teetering sideways, jumping up 1 ½ feet onto the catwalk, spinning and regaining*
my balance before falling off the otherside. Without a lost beat, I continued as if nothing had gone wrong. Everyone was amazed that I had not fallen, and talked about it for weeks."

**The Original, Official DRAG Handbook does not correct
or edit the written responses shared by the performers.
We did not want to change the words in detail in
fear of losing the point the impersonator
was trying to make in their own words.**

Chapter Fifteen Photos: First Image: Idea go / FreeDigitalPhotos.net, Second Image: Salvatore Vuono / FreeDigitalPhotos.net, Third Image: Paul / FreeDigitalPhotos.net, Fourth Image: renjith krishnan / FreeDigitalPhotos.net, Fifth Image: Idea go / FreeDigitalPhotos.net, Sixth Image: Idea go / FreeDigitalPhotos.net,, Seventh Image thegloss.com

**Best Selling Author The Infamous Todd Kachinski Kottmeier
with Steve Hammond and George Summers**

The content of this book came from a survey taken from the author in an attempt to collect details for the second novel, "Turn Around Bright Eyes." The response became so overwhelming that the responses became this book with the first five years of sales donated by the author to charity.

VOTED TOP TEN

"Ways to impress the audience"

10. Wear lots and lots of jewelry

9. Always, remain humble to the audience

8. Do lots and lots of dancing

7. Mingle with the crowd between songs

6. Have high energy during the performance

5. Maintain eye contact with crowd members

4. Wear beautiful makeup

3. Change costumes between songs

2. The bigger the hair the better

1. Knowing the words to your song (47%)

Valentine's Day 2011

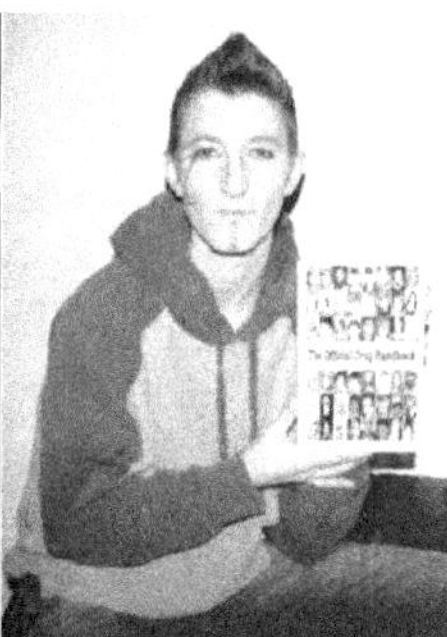

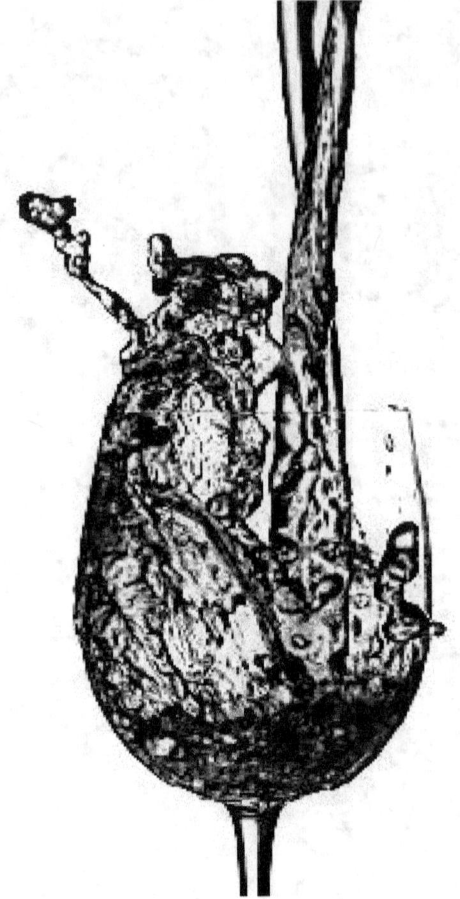

Chapter Sixteen

Bars

Most performers that are new to the business are often under the grand illusion that their talents, charm, and persistent behavior will keep them booked at a bar. For a bar owner, it is about two things, and only those two things; "entertaining my customers to such an extreme, that they are forced to have to return to the bar to see your next performance." Nothing more. Nothing less.

In every jurisdiction of this country, the bar is required by federal law to have an ASCAP or other performing license to use the music played in their bar. This does not mean that the bar has legally fulfilled that obligation. An entertainer approached by a licensing bureau demanding payment for a song that is under copyright (15% of the performers stated they were approached) is not obligated to pay a dime, as it falls within the realm of the venue owner.

Nothing impresses a bar owner more than a female impersonator that enters with a resume of other successful functions, and a built-in following. A new performer doesn't have that advantage. To make up for her inexperience, they must over compensate with enthusiasm. Entering a bar as a performer is the bare minimum required by the manager. The bar manager is not sitting at that table discussing booking shows because they think the performer is the liquor distributor. They are sitting at that table because they think they are interviewing a female impersonator that will impress their customers.

A successful entertainer is also required in today's culture to be a promoter. A female impersonator needs to walk into a bar with an arsenal of ideas to present to the bar owner on marketing themselves. It is no longer the bar owner's sole duties in today's digital age to market their entertainers. Promoting has become the performer's job also.

VOTED TOP TWENTY

"Avenues to promote yourself"

- Facebook
- Twitter
- Text Messaging
- Email
- Calling Friends
- At their real job
- Handing out flyers
- Posters
- MySpace
- Mentioning it at other venues and fundraising*
- Mentioning it while out with friends
- Reminding people at the bar after your performance to return the next week to see you again
- Pageant Tie-Ins
- Begging the bar to cross promote it in their current advertising budget with local periodicals
- Going back to the bar hosting you as a regular customer and to bring friends
- Teaching your partner to network with you as a team
- Begging your friends to network and share the information
- YouTube
- Craig's List Personals
- Constantly reminding yourself all day long what can I do at this moment to convince the people around me to come to my show

Be careful:

I would have freaked out at any performer suggesting to my audience to leave my bar to follow them to my competition!
Todd Kachinski Kottmeier, Retired Restaurant and Bar Owner

Many bar owners have no problem not using successful female impersonators. Often, many bar managers will decide to not use a performer because they bring too much drama, aggravation, or attitude with their makeup kit. I have personally discharged and banned many popular entertainers in my bars because they were not worth the aggravation.

**Top five ways to impress a bar owner,
as voted by bar owners
5. Interacting with customers
4. A drama free area
3. The entertainment factor
2. Someone who will promote
1. Punctuality (62%)**

It is often the grand illusion of female impersonators that the bar has a social obligation or moral conviction for securing the 4,832 items performers DRAG into the dressing room. I can assure you, there is not a single bar that agrees with them.

There are two problems when they bring cool items to work; someone in that dressing room will want it, and someone in that dressing room will steal it. A person that feels they are smarter than the thief, is often proven wrong. Less than 1% of the participants of this book, claim 100% success rate at preventing theft.

A performer coming into the dressing room has 300 things rambling through their minds, while a thief only has one. All the thief needs is that brief moment, that no one is paying attention, to make your cool things their own.

Top Twenty Steps to securing your belongings

❊ ❊ ❊

1. Understand the fact that if someone is going to steal, they are going to steal
2. Leave valuables and unnecessary items in the car
3. Keep suitcases zipped up
4. Keep an eye on it constantly, to let the thief know you are paying attention
5. Only bring things that you need
6. Decline to work at bars that make no effort to protect you. These bars allow open access for their patrons into the dressing room. Bars should be vigilant on posting and enforcing restrictions on open access.
7. Be neat and organized
8. Bring a friend/dresser
9. Make friends with the other performers (like a neighborhood watch)
10. Centralize all of your own belongings
11. Hide high theft items within the luggage
12. Listen to gossip
13. Try to label or mark items for identification
14. Try not to lend items that other people are not responsible to keep safe
15. Clearly label your garment bags and luggage
16. Be nice to people around you, so they don't feel that stealing from you, is good revenge
17. Don't try to impress the room with your belongings
18. Don't borrow without permission
19. Keep uninvited customers out of the dressing room (Don't be afraid to insist that other performers help you keep uninvited guests out of the room) A rule of thumb used by police profilers, "Often, the nicest, most helpful people in the room, are the thieves." <Just saying.>
20. Don't be afraid to use locks

Did you know most of the performers throughout this handbook?

Bonus Material: "Why Me Harvey Milk"
❀ ❀ ❀

Finding your place in the world, your value in the community, and to survive, takes a personal commitment to succeed past obstacles. I want to leave you with some important thoughts. I want you to read the added material I posted in this conclusion of my first Official DRAG Handbook.

This was the first step of a long path for you and me. I need you to make this book a success, displaying wisdom, balancing respect, and displaying the love of the Art. We are following this book with supplemental subjects dedicated to Mentors, Funny Stories, and a host of other subject. Constantly be active with us, and send us your input.

The people this book represents are the foundation of the GLBTQ community. A person that decides to wear that dress, for whatever reason, must be willing to understand that their responsibilities rarely end when the song has played its last note. Every performer interviewed for this book pledged their time and talents to charitable events in their community.

Female and male impersonators (performers) are asked to help fight for a cause, and rarely declined the invitation. It is hard to look in the mirror and believe that you can make a difference in the world. I know this to be true, because I am constantly overwhelmed that anyone would listen to a person like me.

"Why Me,
Harvey Milk?"

Dedication

I dedicate the spirit of this book
David Christopher Bradford
of Brunswick Georgia
(1969 to 1994)

I dedicate my desire to complete this book
to my eldest daughter
Cheryl Ann
who taught me self-forgiveness.

I thank the people of
The Harvey Milk Festival
HarveyMilkFestival.com

To whom this speech was created,
When they invited a simple person like me,
To their first ever, Harvey Milk Festival as both the
Master Of Ceremonies and a Guest Speaker.

Since the publishing of the first edition,
They asked me again to return in 2011 as a Guest Speaker

Why Me,
Harvey Milk?

*A call for you to lead with your heart.
I promise you, your life will follow!*

The Actual Script for the Speech By The Infamous Todd Kachinski
Kottmeier,
Master of Ceremonies of the Historic
First Annual Harvey Milk Festival
May 22, 2010

<Typed out in cadence>

Last week I received an invitation to be a guest speaker and Master of Ceremonies of the Harvey Milk Festival. After I calmed down and excitedly accepted the offer, only one question came to my mind,

"Why me?" I sat there at my desk and I called my daughter. My daughter paused, then only said two words,

"Why you?" Nervously hoping to find some positive validation…

I called my mother. In a most distracted voice she asked,

"Why you?" You see, My glory days of being a mover and shaker are just a far distant memory. I was one of the lucky ones growing up as a young man; rarely did I feel my progression being stopped because I was a gay man.

Yes, I was one of the lucky ones.

I am still one of those lucky ones, but my accomplishments are much like me. They too, are turning gray and now part of the history of Florida's rebellious stages of the eighties and nineties.

I can no longer pick up the local newspapers to revel in the latest activities from "The Twisted Imagination of The Infamous Todd David."
When I moved back home to Florida from Phoenix in November 2009, I was once again just The Infamous Todd Kachinski Kottmeier.

Online, someone asked if, "The Infamous Todd was back."

I had to humbly reply to them, "Only in story book form, my friend, only in story book form."

So once again, I could not shake the feeling of wondering, "Why me?"

Not a week goes by that a person discovering me online, in Florida, since my return, that doesn't remark, in the most sincere of voice,
"Oh my God, Todd, I heard you died a long time ago."

So there I sat inside my empty room, staring at the glow of the computer monitor, perched upon my desk, and said once again, "Why me?"

I am a broken man, far past my prime,
· with a tattered and torn heart from Diluted   Cardiomyopathy,
· looking pretty worn out from a successful battle with AIDS for almost
three decades, · struggling to get past my own insecurities, and now
holding an invitation partake in this historical event.
Again I asked, "Why me?"

Last Sunday I went to church. It is a small Metropolitan Community Church
in Tampa, Florida. I first joined it in 1999 when I was a much more
complicated and successful, young man.

I sat near the front row, right in front of the minister. I bowed my head to
pray as the choir started singing.

The congregation rose for the processional hymn.

I decided at that moment to sneak in a "pre-prayer" to my God. I was
hoping to catch his attention before the rest of the people around me had
a chance to ask for their own agenda.

I needed for a moment... some one-on-one time; a special request!

After all God, I was sitting pretty close to the front of the church, hoping
that had some bearing on the rules of special requests.

I do not know what I thought would happen, but I knew I needed
confidence from someone far stronger then myself.

I stood there in my own self-reflection almost shaking from the fear of my
own manmade insecurities.
My eyes were tightly closed, my arms held each other hugging my chest,
and I could hear my inner thoughts from deep inside me, as I asked my
God one simple question,
"Why me?"

Warm tears welled up in my eyes, catching me off guard, embarrassing me.
My face turning flush against the cold air beating down on me from the
rafters. My thoughts overwhelmed by my own physical disabilities

<Point at each area>

· my scarred face, a lower lip torn from fighting MRSA,· the eleven broken teeth from October's accident still under repair devastating my confidence level,
· the lines and creases carved deep in my face from smiling too much, for far too long,

· the gray in my hair that battles and wins, over the hair dyes I use each month,
· the baldness where my feathered haircuts once flourished,
· the bags and dark circles under my eyes, that reveal the health battles, best kept secret behind closed doors,
· and finally the insecurities that redefined the glimmer, that once sparkled in my eyes.

I could not get past my own image, of how I had become so unattractive over the past few years.

I stood there feeling foolish and alone, in a sanctuary filled with compassionate people.

I stood there in a church that to this day, I still sneak out of, after communion… so people won't talk to me. I leave before the people in my church realized how flawed I had become over the past few years.

<Slowly state the next sentence. This is your quote of the entire speech.>

"It's hard for you to fight for equality, when you look in a mirror and see less of a person looking back at you."

<Longer Pause>

"Why me, dear God, Why Me?"

Now…

<Pause>
I know this is the part of a good story, where the author or speaker explains that a bright light came down to fall upon their face.

Maybe this is the part of the tale where he inspires you, by stating, that the hand of God gently rested upon his shoulder and gave him peace or inspiration.

Perhaps this is the part of the speech where I should be dazzling you, by repeating, that God himself spoke to me, in one of those James Earl Jones voices.

No such luck!

<Pause for hopeful laughter>

My epiphany was not religious last Sunday.

It was actually based on a hilarious thought ...right there, two seconds into the sermon.

I started to smile.

Not just your regular smile, but one of those smiles that people like me, with damaged teeth, try to avoid. I could not reach fast enough for the church bulletin they handed me as I entered the church moments earlier. I pulled a black ink pen from my pocket of my dress pants and started to scribble a note to myself on the information sheet tucked inside its fold.

For you see...

<Slowly start getting more excited and raising your voice>

There was a voice. There was a vision of a man!

My fears instantly, at that moment, vanished. Inside my head, I could picture this simple man. Most likely not known for being to overly attractive himself.

It came from my thoughts of old black and white photos of Harvey Milk.

<Pull out photo of Harvey Milk's face>.
I must admit to you....

I must look you square in the eye and confess... some of those images at that moment were actually publicity photos Academy Award Winner, actor Sean Penn!

Suddenly, with great humor and pleasure, I was picturing Harvey Milk listening to me whine. His simple face looking at me in disbelief.
His meek body,

With his basic smile, sat there in my imagination, making fun of me,
because I thought my looks determined my value on fighting for equality.
For a moment, I had a hard, deep look into Harvey Milk's face.
I began to laugh at my own silliness.

It is in that silliness that I discovered my true value.

Fighting for equality has to be much larger then my own insecurities.

It is much larger than this festival, because, …for this festival to succeed
today …it must last long past the moment you exit this field.

It is much larger then Harvey Milk, …or San Francisco, …or California, …or
this country.

I want to let you in on a secret…

It is not larger than me.
It is not larger than you.
<Start pointing at people in the field>.
It is not larger than you, or you, or you!

Fighting for equality cannot be done alone. It has no expiration date.

It is not a facebook fan page, a MySpace profile, it is not a song, or a story,
or a clever speech.

Fighting for equality is "me" FIGHTING FOR EQUALITY.

Fighting for equality is "you" FIGHTING FOR EQUALITY.

Harvey Milk reminded us, that we can all make a difference, if we can all
look beyond our own fears and vacillation to work together.

· In that brief second in church, Harvey Milk reminded me,
< be silly>

"with his own image," **<hold up Harvey Milk's photo again>**

that, …
· "You don't need to be the prettiest person in the room to fight for
equality."

· "You don't need to be the smartest person in the room to fight for equality."
· "You don't need to be the most popular individual
in any room to fight for equality."
· And believe me, "You don't need to be the best speaker to fight for equality."

The only demand we need to place upon ourselves is the desire to stand up, to be counted, as one LOUD voice, demanding that equality includes all of us.

Harvey Milk taught us that fighting for equality forces us to look, far beyond ourselves, and our roles in society.
For a moment we cannot be White, we cannot be Black, Asian, and Hispanic...

nor even Men or Women.

We cannot be Democrats, Republicans, Christians, Jews, or Pagans...

or even Straight or Gay.
When you can look beyond your label,

look beyond the conformity of society ...
look beyond yourself ... then you will realize that none of us are completely equal until the person next to you is "unconditionally equal."

For the definition of equality, by its very nature, requires nothing less.

Nobody is equal until everybody is equal!

I can promise you, that nowhere during my research for this festival, did I find a single sentence where Harvey Milk implied that he was leading us to the Promised Land.

Harvey Milk was simply the caretaker of the key to the door, that he HELPED open for the rest of us to walk through.

Harvey Milk's sudden death did not end our march. For his steps, my friends, were just the beginning.
He did not live his life for us to stop fighting for equality just because he was not present.

For you to make a change in the world, you must believe that his intentions, his path and his spirit were nothing less then your own.

It is our challenge to continue that momentum, to never look at yourself as the victim, and to never consider your role in life as too insignificant to matter.

Nothing will be accomplished, if each of us continues to question, "Why me?"

When you wake up each morning, if you catch yourself looking into that mirror and wondering, "Why me?"... I challenge you to reply "Why not!"

<Start increasing your voice and enthusiasm level for the next section>

When you are living each day and wondering, "Why me?" then I challenge you to reply "Why not!" If you go to bed at night, and you find yourself wondering, "Why me?" then I challenge you to reply

"Why not!" Once you can learn to believe, you can make a difference, then you will begin to hear yourself volunteer, to join others in the fight for equality,

"Pick me!" *<Slam your chest>*
"Pick me, to fight your battles!"
"Pick me, to be your strength!"
"Pick me, to stand beside you!"
"Pick me!   Pick me!
<quieter>

"Pick me."

Look around you! Look at all the talent. Feel the energy of this crowd.
Adore the compassion of the people around you.
Relate to this cause.

Look around you! You are part of a gang, a movement, a crowd, a loud voice defining this moment in your life. You have become, without realizing it, part

of the enthusiasm and momentum needed for change.
Look around you!
<Drop voice level to almost a whisper>

For a moment, look around you.
If for a moment you can think, "Wow, there are a lot of good people here today" then remember, "These are the same people thinking that of you."
<Speak at normal tone>

At this moment people in this field are looking at you too.

They are standing next to you, they are standing behind you,
they are the talented artists here today to entertain you, they are your friends, that share your laughter and your tears,

they are your teachers, they are the people that drive next to you,
they are the nurses that mend you when you are sick, and
they include the people in this field, that you have not met ...YET ...in your life.
All of these people, at this moment, are looking back at you.
Look around you!

All week long, I asked thousands of people online to remember today.
Today I ask you, "What did you do at this moment on May 22, 1990, TEN YEARS AGO?"

"What did you do, in detail, on that day ten years ago?"

<Point at someone in the crowd>
What did you do?
I don't have the slightest clue what I did ten years ago today.

For the rest of your life, until the day you take your last breath, you will remember today.
Think about the importance of that sentence.

You will remember that you, were in attendance, on the first ever, Harvey Milk Festival in Sarasota, Florida, on this day, in 2010. For the... rest... of ... your life.

For the rest of your life you will be able to know, that you were offered a chance today, to help make a difference in your life... and in his life... and in her life

I hope today that we can influence you to leave this festival marked with messages, …with information, …with a personal desire to help "each other" by becoming a single voice demanding for equality.

I want you to leave this field today with a plan for tomorrow.

Today cannot be confused as another day you spent at the bar.

Today will not be just another day, tanning by the water or even confused as one of the days you sat safely on your couch watching TV. Today will not be confused with any other day in your entire life.

It is what you desire to do with today
TOMORROW
That will determine all of our destinies.
Today we ask you to open your heart.
Today we ask you to open your mind.

Listen to the messages we share together, so the next time you are alone sitting by yourself in a room and someone asks you for help, you don't have to say, "Why me."

My name is (Enter your name here).

Pick me.

Ten Black Books

Book 1 DRAG411's
"DRAG Bully, A Survivor's Guide"

The Largest Bullying Project in LGBT History for Struggling Entertainers. Advice from over a hundred male, female, and androgynous impersonators around the world to help entertainers struggling with their family, peers, relationships, neighbors, regular jobs, venues, and successfully overcoming self-doubt. Best Selling author Todd Kachinski Kottmeier created DRAG411 to document the lives of male, female, and androgynous impersonator years ago. It is now the largest organization for impersonators on earth with over 7,000 entertainers in 32 countries. DRAG411 also operates The International Original, Official DRAG Memorial with almost a thousand names (2018). This is his 25th book, 20th World Record, and 12th book on this subject. Thousands of invitations to contribute were send out. This book contains the best of their responses, in their own words, to you.

Book 2 DRAG411's
"Original DRAG Handbook"

Over 155 female impersonators (and 1 male impersonator) from around the world share over a thousand insightful comments in the first handbook created of this art form.

Commentary shared with Todd Kachinski Kottmeier included the following contributors of The Original, DRAG Handbook to include Ada Buffet, Adora , Adrian Leigh, Afeelya Bunz, Alisa Summers, Alanna Divine, Alexis De La Mer, Alexis Mateo, Alex Serpa, Allure, Amanda Bone, Amanda Love, Amy DeMilo, Anastaia Fallon, Astasnaia Rexia, Angel gLamar, Angela Dodd, Anita Cox, April Fresh, Ashleigh Cooley, Aurora Sexton, Babette Schwartz, Bailey St. James, Barbra Herr, Barbra Seville, Beverly LaSalle, BJ Stephens, Blair Michaels, Brandon M. Caten, Brianna Lee, Brittany Moore, Brookyln Bisette, Bukkake Blaque London St. James, Cartier Paris, Cathy Craig, Champagne T. Bordeaux, Cherry Darling, Christina Paris, CoCo LaBelle, CoCo Montrese, CoCo St. James, Conundrum, Crystal Belle, Daniel Murphy, Danika Fierce, Daphne Ferraro, Dasha Nicole, Dee Gregory, Deva DaVyne, Diamond Dunhill, Diedra Windsor Walker, Dmentia Divinyl/Eva LaDeva, Echo Dazz, Esme Russell, Estelle Rivers, Eunyce Raye, Felica Fox, Felina Cashmere, Geraldine Queen Cabaret, Ginger Minj, Glitz Glam, Gilda Golden, Horchata, Ima Twat, Ineeda Twat, Jade Daniels, Jade Jolie, Jade Shanell, Jade Sotomayo, Jaeda Fuentes, Jami Micheals, Jay Santana, Jeffrey Powell, Jenna Chambers Tisdale, Jessica Jade, Jocelyn Summers, Jodie Holliday, Joey Brooks, Joshua Myers, J.P. Patrick, Juwanna Jackson, Kamden Wells, Katrina Starr, Kenny Braverman, Khrystal Leight, Kier Sarkesian, Kiki LaFlare Santangilo, Kitty D'Meaner, Kori Stevens, Krystal Amore Adonis, Lacey Lynn Taylors, Lady Clover Honey, Lady Sabrina, Lady TaJma Hall, Lakeisha Pryce, LeeAnna Love, Leigh Shannon, Lisa Carr, Lola Honey, Madisyn De La Mer, Makayla Rose Devine,

Maxine Padlock (Maxi Pad), Melissa Morgan, Melody Mayheim, Michael Wilson, Mike Astermon-Glidden, Mis Sadistic, Miss Conception, Miss Gigi, Mr. Kenneth Blake, Misty Eyez, Monique Michaels, Myah Monroe, Mystique Summers, Nairobi V. D'Viante, Naomi D-Lish, Naomi Wynters, Nicole Paige Brooks, Nikki Dynamite, Nova Starr, Ororo, Patrica Grand, Patricia Knight, Patrica Mason, Pandora DeStrange, Penelope Reigns, Polly FunkChanel, Phiore Star Liemont, Purrzsa Kyttyn, Pussy LeHoot, Raquel Payne, Rhyana Vorhman, Rickie Lee, Rusti Fawcett, Scarlett Fever, Selina Kyle, Shae Shae LaReese, Shealita Babay, Shugah Caine, Stephanie Roberts, Stephanie Stuart, Stormy Vain, Summer Breeze, Sybil Storm, Tabatha Lovall, Tatum Michelle, Teri Courtney, Tiffani Middlesexx, Timm McBride, Toni Davyne, TotiYanah Diamond,Trixie LaRue, Trixie Pleasures, Vegas Platinum, Venus D Lite, Vivika D'Angelo, Wendel Duppert and Wendy G. Kennedy.

Book 3:   DRAG411's
"Crown Me! Winning Pageants"

Hundreds of invitations sent to the titleholders, pageant promoters, judges, and talent show hosts to share their insight on not only winning pageants and contests but also owning the stage every time they perform. Their topics included auxiliary steps to success needed for song selection, dancing, movement on stage, props, backup dancers, creating your own edge, personal interviews, steps to success for winning the talent category every time you step on stage, on stage questions, eveningwear, and creative costuming. They discussed in their own unedited words, wardrobe changes, makeup, hair, shoes, when is the time to compete, qualities needed for a judge, and the top misconceptions of contestants competing in the pageantry systems.

Commentary shared with Todd Kachinski Kottmeier included the following contributors of Crown Me! to include AJ Menendez, Amy Demilo, Anastacia Dupree, Anson Reign, Bob Taylor, Breonna Tenae, Brittany T Moore, Coco Montrese, Dana Douglas, Darryl Kent, Denise Russell, Dey Jzah Opulent, Freddy Prinze Charming, Gage Gatlyn, Jay Santana , Jayden Knight, Jennifer Foxx, Joey Jay, Kori Stevens, Mis Sadistic, Mykul Jay Valentine, Natasha Richards, Rico Taylor, Sam Hare, Stephanie Stuart, Taina T. Norell, Tiffani Middlesexx, Tori Taylor, Ty Nolan, Vinnie Marconi, and Vivika D'Angelo.

Book 4:   DRAG411's
"DRAG King Guide"

Over 155 male impersonators around the world share over a thousand insightful comments in forty-one chapters.

Commentary shared with Todd Kachinski Kottmeier included the following contributors of The Official DRAG King and Male Impersonators Guide to include Aaron Phoenix, Abs Hart, Adam All, Adam DoEve, AJ Menendez, Alec Allnight, Alexander Cameron, Alik Muf, Andrew Citino, Anjie Swidergal, Anson Reign, Ashton The Adorable Lover, Atown, Ayden Layne, B J Armani, B J Bottoms, Bailey Saint James, Ben Doverr, Ben Eaten, Bootzy Edwards Collynz, Brandon KC Young-Taylor, Bruno Diaz, Cage Masters, Campbell Reid Andrews, Chance Wise, Chandler J Hart, Chasin Love, Cherry Tyler Manhattan, Chris Mandingo, Clark Kunt, Clint Torres, Cody Wellch Klondyke, Colin Grey, Corey James Caster, Coti Blayne, Crash Bandikok, Dakota Rain, Dante Diamond, Davion Summers, DeVery Bess, Devin G. Dame, Devon Ayers, Dionysus W Khaos, Diseal Tanks Roberts, D-Luv Saviyon, Dominic Demornay, Dominic Von Strap, D-Rex, Dylan Kane, E. M. Shaun, Eddie C. Broadway, Emilio, Erick LaRue, Flex Jonez, Freddy Prinze Charming, Gabe King, Gage Gatlyn, George De Micheal,

Greyson Bolt, Gunner Gatlyn, Gus Magendor, Hawk Stuart, Harry Pi, Holden Michael, Howie Feltersnatch, Hurricane Savage, J Breezy St James, Jack E. Dickinson, Jack King, Jake Van Camp, Jamel Knight, Jenson C. Dean, Johnnie Blackheart, Jonah Godfather of DRAG, Jordan Allen, Jordan Reighn, Joshua K. Mann, Joshua Micheals, Juan Kerr, Julius M. SeizeHer, Jude Lawless, Justin Cider, Justin Luvan, Justin Sider, K'ne Cole, Kameo Dupree, Kenneth J. Squires, King Dante, King Ramsey, Jack Inman, Kody Sky, Koomah, Kristian Kyler, Kruz Mhee, Linda Hermann-Chasin, Luke Ateraz, Lyle Love-It, Macximus, Marcus Mayhem, Marty Brown, Master Cameron Eric Leon, Max Hardswell, MaXx Decco, Michael Christian, Mike Oxready, Miles Long, Mr-Charlie Smith, Nanette D'angelo Sylvan, Nolan Neptune, Orion Blaze Browne, Owlejandro Monroe, Papa Cherry, Papi Chulo, Papi Chulo Doll, Persian Prince, Phantom, Pierce Gabriel, Rasta Boi Punany, Rico M Taylor, Rock McGroyn, Rocky Valentino, Rogue DRAG King, Romeo Sanchez, Rychard "Alpha" Le'Sabre, Ryder Knightly, Ryder Long, Sam Masterson, Sammy Silver, Santana Romero, Scorpio, Shane Rebel Caine, Shook ByNature, Silk Steele Prince, SirMandingo Thatis, Smitty O'Toole, Soco Dupree, Spacee Kadett, Starr Masters, Stefan LeDude, Stefon Royce Iman, Stefon SanDiego, Stormm, Teddy Michael, Thug Passion, Travis Luvermore, Travis Hard, Trey C. Michaels, Trigger Montgomery, Tyler Manhattan, Viciouse Slick, Vinnie Marconi, Welland Dowd, William Vanity Matrix, Wulf Von Monroe, Xander Havoc, and Xavier Bottoms.

Book 5:   DRAG411's
"DRAG Stories"

Funny stories shared with Todd Kachinski Kottmeier including the following contributors of DRAG Stories to include Chance Wise, Anson Reign, Tiffani Middlesexx, Rico Taylor, Todd Kachinski Kottmeier, Bob Taylor, Stefon Royce Iman, Candi Samples, Alexis Mateo, Naomi Wynters, Dmentia Divinyl, Bruce Lacie, Kennedy Wendy, Chastity Rose, Miss GiGi, Angel gLamar, Patricia Grand, Shook ByNature, Lady Guy, Eunyce Raye, Charley Marie Coutora, Jezzie Bell, Lamar Kellam, Jayden St. James, Rachelle Ann Summers, Champagne T Bordeaux, Gilda Golden, Daisha Monet, Vivika D'Angelo, Rachel Boheme, Esme Rodriguez, and MaNu Da Original.

Book 6:   DRAG411's
"DRAG Mother, DRAG Father" Honoring Mentors

Performers look to DRAG mothers, DRAG fathers, friends, and fans for insight, compassion, and guidance as mentors. This book honors those special people. Over 140 entertainers contributed wisdom and words for this historical book, making it the largest project of its nature in GLBTQ history and the first published book on male and female mentors.

Commentary shared with Todd Kachinski Kottmeier included the following contributors of DRAG Parents to includee AJ Menendez, Vinnie Marconi, Mis Sadistic, Todd Kachinski Kottmeier, Bob Taylor, Taina Norell, Andrew Stratton, Horchata Horchata, David Warner, Gianna Love, Trinity Taylor, Domunique Jazmin Vizcaya, Brittany Moore, PurrZsa Kyttyn, Jake Lickus, Shelita Taylor, Adriana Manchez, MiMi Welch, China Taylor, Armondis Bone't, Monique Trudeau, Simeon Codfish, Diamond Dupree, Stefon Royce Iman, Jayden Stjames, Demonica da Bomb, Colin Grey, Christopher Todd Guy, Celyndra Lashay Clyne, Candice St. James, Justin Barnes Williams, Ivanna Dooche, London Taylor Douglas, Christina Alexandria Victoria Regina Lowe, Bianca DeMonet, Critiqa Mann, Jazmen Andrews, AJ Allen, TotiYanah Diamond, D' Marco Knight, Chip Matthews, Mirage Montrese, India Starr Simms, Jade S Stratton, Emerald Divine, Elysse Giovanni, Vanity Halston, Kristofer Reynolds, Akasha Uravitch, Adriana Fuentes, Erykah Mirage, Felicity Ferraro, Joey Payge, Rhiannon Todd, Vicious Slick, Amirage Saling, Tori Sass, Chy'enne Valentino, and Robbi Lynn.

Book 7: DRAG411's
"Spotlight Today"

It was the World's Largest Paperback Magazine for Impersonators and Fans when it premiered with over 175 pages. DRAG411 no longer prints Spotlight Today Magazine, but here is the re-release of the groundbreaking first edition. Complete articles by Vinnie Marconi, Denise Russell, Tiffani T. Middlesexx, Kristofer Reynolds, Magenta Alexandria Dupree, Butch Daddy, Vivikah Kayson-Raye, Makanoe, Amanda Lay, Thomas DeVoyd, Kevin B. Reed, Glenn Storm, and over 150 impersonators from around the world.

Book 8:   DRAG411's
"DRAG Queen Guide"

Almost two hundred female impersonators around the world share over a thousand insightful comments in forty-one chapters.

Commentary shared with Todd Kachinski Kottmeier included the following contributors of Official DRAG Queen and Female Impersonator Handbook to include Alana Summers, Alexis Marie Von Furstenburg, Alize', Aloe Vera, Alysin Wonderland, Amanda Bone DeMornay, Amanda Lay, Amanda Roberts, Amy DeMilo, Anastasia Fallon, Angie Ovahness, Anita Mandinite, Appolonia Cruz, Ashlyn Tyler, Aurora Tr'Nele Michelle, Azia Sparks, Barbie Dayne, Barbra Herr, Beverly LaSalle, Bianca DeMonet, Bianca Lynn Breeze, Blair Michaels, Boxxa Vine, Brittany T Moore, Britney Towers, Brandi Amara Skyy, Brooke Lynn Bradshaw, Candi Samples, Candi Stratton, Candy Sugar, Cathy Craig, Catia Lee Love, CeCe Georgia, Cee-Cee LaRouge-Avalon, Celeste Starr, Chad Michaels, Chevon Davis, Cheyenne Desoto Mykels, Chi Chi Lalique, Christina Collins, Chrystal Conners, Claudia B Eautiful, Coca Mesa, Coco St James, Damiana LaRoux, Dana Scrumptious, Danyel Vasquez, Dee Gregory, Delores T. Van-Cartier, Demonica DaBaum, Denise Russell, Diamond Dunhill, Diva Lilo, Diva Savage, Dove, EdriAna Treviño, Elle Emenopé, Elysse Giovanni, Erica James, Esmé Rodríguez, Estella Sweet, Eunyce Raye, Eva Nichole Distruction, Faleasha Savage, Felicia Minor, Felicity Frockaccino, Gigi Masters, Ginger Alley, Ginger Gigi Diamond, Ginger Kaye Belmont, Glitz Glam, Grecia Montes D' Occa, Heather Daniels, Hennessy Heart, Hershae Chocolatae, Holy McGrail, Hope B Childs, Horchata, India Brooks, India Ferrah, Ivy Profen, Izzy Adahl, Jaclyn St James, Jade Iroq, Jade Sotomayor, Jade Taylor Stratton, Jamie-Ree Swan, Jennifer Warner, Jessica Brooks, Jexa Ren'ae Van de Kamp, Joey Brooks, Jonny Pride, Kamelle Toe, Karma Jayde Addams, Kelly Turner, Mama Savannah Georgia, Mr. Kenneth Blake, Kamden T. Rage, Kira Stone-St James, Kirby Kolby, Kita Rose, Krysta Radiance, Lacie Bruce, Lady Jasmine Michaels, Lady Pearl, Lady Sabrina, Latrice Royale, LaTonga Manchez, Leona Barr, Lexi Alexander, Lilo Monroe, Lindsay Carlton, Lucinda Holliday, Lunara Sky, Lupita Chiquita Michaels Alexander, Madam Diva Divine, Mahog Anny, Makayla Michelle Davis Diamond, Mariah Cherry, Maxine Padlock, Melody Mayheim, Menaje E'toi, Mercede Andrews, Mi$hal, Mia Fierce, Michelle Leigh Sterling, Miss Diva Savage, Miss GiGi, Misty Eyez, Mitze Peterbilt, Monica Mystique, Montrese Lamar Hollar, Morgana DeRaven, Muffy Vanbeaverhousen, Natasha Richards, Nathan Loveland, Nicole Paige Brooks, Nikki Garcia, Nostalgia Todd Ronin, Olivia St James, Paige Sinclair, Pandora DeCeption,

Pheobe James, Reia'Cheille Lucious, Robyn Demornay, Robyn Graves, Rhonda Sheer, Rose Murphy, Ruby Diamond NY, Ruby Holiday, Ryan Royale, Rychard "Alpha" Le'Sabre, Rye Seronie, Sable Monay, Sabrina Kayson-Raye, Samantha St Clair, Sanaa Raelynn, Sapphire T. Mylan, Sasha Phillips, Savannah Rivers, Savannah Stevens, Selina Kyle, Sha'day Halston-St James, ShaeShae LaReese, Shamya Banx, Shana Nicole, Shaunna Rai, Sierra Foxx White, Sierra Santana, Sonja Jae Savage, Stella D'oro, Strawberry Whip, Sugarpill, Tasha Carter, Tanna Blake, Taquella Roze, Tawdri Hipburn, Taylor Rockland, Tempest DuJour, Tiffani T. Middlesexx, Traci Russell, Trudy Tyler, Vanessa del Rey, Velveeta WhoreMel, Vera Delmar, Vicky Summers, Vita DeVine, Vivian Sorensin, Vivian Von Brokenhymen, Vivika D'Angelo-Steele, Wendy G. Kennedy, Willmuh Dickfit, Wynter Storm, Yasmine Alexander and ZuZu Bella.

Book 9: DRAG411's (Two Comedy Scripts)
"Best Said Dead" and **"Following Wynter"**

Best Said Dead examines in funny conversations those brief minutes after a person dies. Many religions and beliefs define different paths for each of us. Rarely do we discuss those precious moments between death and the final destination. This comedy opens the possibilities that for a moment, a person vanishes into the memories in their mind. Any part can be male, female, or ambiguous.

Following Wynter is a hilarious comedy play. Ethan discovers his newlywed husband is the flamboyant DRAG queen Wynter Storm in this whimsical farce with an important message of believing in yourself and your friends. . . even if your friend is Serena Silver. Any part can be male, female, or ambiguous.

Book 10:   DRAG411's
"DRAG World"
The contributing writers of DRAG411's "Spotlight Magazine," the World's Largest Paperback Magazine for Impersonators and Fans when it premiered in 2012 with over 175 pages, created this companion book. DRAG411 no longer prints Spotlight Today Magazine, but above you will find Book 7 is the re-release of the groundbreaking first edition. Complete chapters on DRAG Marketing by DRAG411.

Complimentary articles on Confidence, Duct Tape, Music Selection, Living Divinely, authentic stage presence, Pageants, having fun performing, jewelry, legislative information from the United States and around the world, the Old School performers, Virgin stage performers, and payday from contributing writers including Denise Russell, Jay Santana, Chance Wise,

Vivikah Kayson-Raye, AJ Menedez, Glenn Storm, Freddy Prinze Charming, Gage Gatlyn, Kevin B. Reed, and over 100 impersonators from around the world!

Other books from the Best Selling author
The Infamous **Todd Kachinski Kottmeier**

"Turn Around Bright Eyes, The DRAG Queen Killer"

Few crimes in gay history rocked a nation as great as The DRAG Queen Killer. The country seemed paralyzed from the first ring of the chain tapping on the concrete, as they pulled Cassandra to her death, until the very last brutal killing. The murderous rampage seemed buried amongst the media suffering from a barrage of tales from the 9-11 terrorist attacks.

"CommUnity of Transition"

We sent over a thousand invitations to the transgender community around the world asking them to share wisdom, advice, and compassion for those questioning or struggling. No restraints, using topics they created, as they guided the conversation over forty chapters and fifty topics. By the close, these remarkable people had created the largest compilation book in transgender history. They opened their heart with these words.

NOTE: *This book is "lightly edited" to reflect the intent and form of over one hundred transgender contributors. Unedited photographs "before and after" come from actual contributing transgender writers.*

"Joey Brooks, The Show Must Go On"
By Joey Brooks and Todd Kachinski Kottmeier

Joey Brooks, The Show Must Go On is the story of The First Lady of Ybor from the days of El Goya to present day. Female Impersonator, Show director, hostess, author…
"Old school, new school, no school… who gives a shit? I'm too old to go to school. I barely remember last week. When I get too old to remember what the fuck I did when I was young …ger, I'll just open one of these books and laugh my ass off. I wonder how many other queens had this much fun becoming one of the icons of their community. Too funny. I just called myself an icon. Hell, I must be a queen. Only a female impersonator could call themselves a diva, a queen, a star without people giggling behind her back. Giggling is good. A twenty-dollar bill is better."

"Two Days Past Dead"

The Author's First Published Book

It is hard to be the good guy when you succeed so well being bad. This is the Auggie Summer's dilemma his entire life. The story, based loosely on the tales of The Infamous Todd, follows the precocious child. His story begins with selling candy in 9th grade where he catches not only the attention of the press but also amusement of the drug cartel early in its' own infancy. Auggie Summers finds himself in the forefront of one of the most dangerous organizations on Earth.

"Waiting On God"
The Author's Humorist Novel

Learn to live after the doctors tell you "that are dying." A humorist essay on embracing funny moments and to create an environment around you that makes people not only laugh, but also be inspired by your strength.